DATE DUE

COMMUNICATION IN THE COUNSELING RELATIONSHIP

COMMUNICATION

IN THE COUNSELING RELATIONSHIP

BONNIE JAY HEADINGTON

THE CARROLL
PRESS
Publishers

43 Squantum St., Cranston, R. I. 02920

About the Author —

BONNIE JAY HEADINGTON is Associate Professor of Psychology at Humboldt State University in Arcata, California. She has taught a variety of courses including techniques of individual and group therapy. A licensed practicing psychologist in California, she is a staff trainer and consultant for numerous agencies and institutions. Her background includes supervision and training of counselors and teachers, elementary and junior high school teaching and work with handicapped children and adults.

Dr. Headington is a member of the American Psychological Association, American Personnel and Guidance Association, Association for Counselor Education and Supervision and the Western Association for Counselor Education and Supervision. She received her Ph.D. degree in counseling from Ohio University and is the mother of two children.

Library of Congress Cataloging in Publication Data

Headington, Bonnie Jay

Communication in the counseling relationship.

Bibliography: p.
Includes index.
1. Counseling. 2. Interpersonal communication.
I. Title.
BF637.C6H37   158   78-9026

ISBN 0-910328-24

THE CARROLL PRESS
Publishers
43 Squantum Street
Cranston, Rhode Island 02920

Manufactured in the United States of America

CONTENTS

iii

CONTENTS – *continued*

INTRODUCTION

Why Counseling?

Counseling as a career is attracting more and more persons to its ranks. Its advantages as a profession are appealing. To the naive observer it is a way of solving the world's problems in a direct, meaningful manner, a way of helping humanity, and a method of becoming involved with people in a personal way. This magical, attractive contact with others has developed in a variety of ways throughout the professional history of counseling.

Counseling and psychotherapy belong to one large field with roots in many traditions. The original healers of the mind came from a religious/mystical background. Medicine contributed its share of healers: In fact, the tradition of the medical model of doctor-patient was so pervasive that many of the giants of psychology were physicians first (e. g., Freud, Fromm-Reichman) and specialized in matters of the mind. Psychotherapy is in some ways today still dominated by the profession of psychiatry, which requires a medical degree. Psychology as a separate, but obviously related tradition, contributed its leaders to the helping profession spurred by the growth of the mental-health movement in the United States. In 1908 a former mental health patient, Clifford Beers wrote a remarkable book called *A Mind That Found Itself* which described conditions in mental hospitals and focused national attention on the problems of mental illness. The other significant thread in American counseling stems from Frank Parsons, who in 1909 wrote a book which stimulated interest in guidance and counseling as a necessary part of choosing a vocation. The expansion of guidance services from career choice to a plethora of decision-making processes extended guidance into the schools. Half a century later, school counseling expanded again, both horizontally (more and better services) and vertically (college downward into the elementary schools) as a result of an "outside" historical event: the Sputnik launching by the Russians. The national effort to catch up, match and beat the Soviets in the "space race" focused attention on the scientific lag in our public schools. Congressional funding, under the National Defense Education Act, was designed to assist the identification, guidance and education of gifted youth and, as such provided incentive (and funding) for meeting the educational needs of all students through more and better counseling and guidance services.

Interest in school counseling has declined somewhat since that peaking, yet the incidence of troubled youth in our schools has not declined. Counselors and guidance workers are still needed in this setting.

Counselors and psychotherapists* are still needed in the community as well. The same critical societal factors which causally contribute to troubled youth in our schools causally contribute to troubled individuals in our communities.

One of the largest problems in American society has been a sense of isolation, perhaps fostered by the growth of cities, the increased impact of industrialization and the technological advances and the lowered influence of the nuclear family. In many ways, the school has assumed many of the responsibilities in our society that the nuclear family and the extended family have been unable to meet. In the modern-day absence of aunts, uncles, grandparents, youngsters often seek out adults within the school setting (teachers and counselors) to trust. Partially reflecting this trend and partially reflecting the contributions of the growth of the mental health movement, the school system hires counselors to help youngsters with educational, career and vocational choices, decision making and personal problems.

Isolation does not seem to be limited to children and adolescents. In a world where personal significance seems to be harder and harder to achieve, alienation and a lack of a feeling of relatedness seem to be the norm, rather than the exception. Frequently the need for meaningful contact is what propels many adults into the counseling relationship.

It can be hypothesized that this same need is what propels many adults into the idea of counseling as a career choice. More and more persons are simply seeking the kind of career where they can relate effectively to others. This may involve any one of several careers which are classified under the term "the helping professions." And, because the helping professions involve careers ranging from nursing, social work, education, and psychology to employment counselors and business administrators in personnel management fields, the helping professions are a multi-faceted jewel with a generally basic goal — that of one person assisting another.

---

*   The two terms are often used to denote the difference in traditions: The label "counselor" stems from the guidance movement and work in public settings such as schools and colleges; "psychotherapists" are seen as working in clinical settings such as hospitals, private practice and mental health clinics. As I received training in both traditions, I have never been able to make such arbitrary distinctions. For me, the difference between the two has been in the severity of the client's problems — the more severe problems are usually seen in the psychotherapy model setting.

Counseling is therefore defined as a process in which one person who is supposedly more skilled is assisting another person to cope effectively with the problems of life. Problems of living may include developmental life stages, vocational choice, marital discord, changes in life style and the myriad of difficulties which beset us all on our way through the time space from birth to death.

It is counseling's humanitarian aspect, appropriate or inappropriate as that may be, which is probably most appealing and most attractive to the person who is considering counseling as a career choice, who is committed to counseling as a profession or who is just plain *curious* about the field.

There are obviously reasons other than altruism which contribute to an individual choosing counseling as a career. The influence and heritage of Parsons and the vocational guidance movement would suggest that counselors may need to examine their own motivations critically so that personal knowledge combined with more realistic views of an exceedingly difficult profession will assist them in making a wise career decision. This book attempts to help you, the reader, in both of those processes.

The following chapters will not teach you how to counsel another person. That is a mixture of skill and art which each of you must try on and adapt to your own style — your own personal sense of who and what you are. But the methodology which follows will teach you what to do in several situations, what *not* to do, and how to hear yourself as well as your client. The purpose in this book is to pull together from several sources some of what has been learned about counseling, present it in a systematic way, and allow you to try it on. It is hoped that it makes sense to you and gives you: (1) a better basis for understanding your communication with others, (2) a better basis for knowing "about" counseling, and (3) the incentive to find out more. This book is conceived as a beginning. Hopefully, you will add the necessary layers of knowledge of human behavior, personality theories, psychodynamics and experience with people to become a counselor.

Use of the Text

The following chapters have been designed for use in an introductory counseling skills class. The class wherein this text was developed has approximately thirty students and meets seven hours a week. The class as a whole meets with the instructor for one hour for an explanation of the assignment and a demonstration of the skill to be acquired during that week. The class is divided into three groups of equal size which remain intact for the quarter/semester.

Two hours are devoted to practice and making the assigned audio or video tapes; two hours are spent as a group doing the assigned group exercises; and two hours are spent playing the tapes for the instructor and for each other. The focus during the latter two hours is on discussion and feedback. If necessary, the skills can be re-taught and an additional practice tape can be made. However, it should be noted that the students have each other as models in this sort of an arrangement and backtracking is rarely necessary. This format, of course, can be adapted to the specific needs and wishes of any instructor and class so long as the basic sequence — modeling and explanation, practice and related exercises, playback and corrective feedback — is maintained. Considerable emphasis, obviously, is placed throughout the sequence on communication — between instructor/student, between and among students in a one-to-one setting, and in the group. This laboratory method has been an effective way of increasing communication skills among prospective counselors.

It is generally accepted that the best way to learn is by doing. The debate which is most frequently stimulated by laboratory experiences is whether it is best to learn within the relative safety of the laboratory or out-there in the "real" world. The position taken here is that the laboratory is a place to *begin to learn*. The safety of the laboratory is not just a consideration for the beginning counselor but perhaps for the clients as well. There has been some concern expressed in the literature over the ethical considerations and ramifications of using untrained counselors paired with clients who are seeking assistance and who are in various stages of difficulties. The problems posed by taping, playing the tapes for small groups of students and a supervisor, perfecting techniques and skills frequently outweigh the importance of the helping relationship to be formed between counselor and client. While all these exercises are going on, the client would still like some assistance with whatever problems s/he has brought to the counseling session. It is suggested that perhaps the laboratory experience can provide a basic understanding of the counseling process, the nature of interpersonal interaction and a backlog of counseling skills which will enable the beginning counselor to meet a "real" client on more secure footing. The paradox here is that even a practice counseling session with another student can generate the same possibilities for meaningful interaction. The same communication processes occur and the same skills prove to be helpful in fostering the relationship. There is a certain reality even to a practice interview. The safety factor that is provided by a team effort — working with one's peers, making similar mistakes — keeps that reality from becoming overwhelming. It also seems valid to experience both roles — acting as both counselor and as client, which provide definite differences in perceiving the relationship.

Organization of the Book

Many chapters are organized into three sections. The first part covers a particular skill or set of skills and some of the rationale supporting their usage. The next section contains the practice exercises and activities using those skills. Some of the activities are designed to provide practical understanding of the rationale behind each skill. Finally, the last section in these chapters covers some suggested additional readings which will aid the reader in gaining further understanding of the skills and the processes involved at each stage of skill acquisition.

The book itself is also organized into three sections. The first section focuses on interactions which occur primarily in the beginning stages of the counseling relationship. These interactions and counseling responses are based on the *content* of what is being said. The counselor, during *level one* or content interactions, is asked to develop his/her listening skills and to attend to the message in what is being said. The counselor is trained to refocus his/her attention on the speaker and away from concerns about what s/he could say to add to the conversation.

The second section of the book focuses on interactions which occur as the counseling relationship develops and as the client explores his/her concerns and life space in increasing depth. The emotional message which is an integral part of any content becomes more apparent at this level of communication. The major portion of material a counselor works with is how the client feels about what is being expressed. The counselor is asked to increase sensitivity to the range and variety of the client's emotional experience.

The third section of the book suggests that a third, deeper level of feeling exists between counselor and client and in the client's relationship to him/herself. This core level of experiencing influences and frequently distorts the counseling relationship. Messages are often noticeably unclear; the words expressed may reflect more of the feelings the speaker has about the relationship and him/herself than the feelings held about the subject itself. The counselor is asked to increase sensitivity to the counselor's own emotional responses within the relationship and how her/his own feelings may be clues to the dynamics of the interaction as well as to the nature of the client's difficulties.

Those three levels of communication comprise an arbitrary way of organizing counselor responses within a relationship and a view of the progression of a growing counseling relationship. There have been many theoretical descriptions of the client who is in difficulty. The premise and organizing principle of this book is that the client is more usefully viewed *within the counseling relationship*. The client did not develop his/her problems in a vacuum; the client will not communicate about his/her problems in a vacuum and the client will certainly not resolve them or work them through alone. Counseling, therefore, is a special kind of communication between two people with the stated purpose of assisting one person with resolution.

* * * * *

ACKNOWLEDGEMENTS

Examination of the communication process in counseling is not a new idea but I have attempted to synthesize the elements of communication that I believe to be both the "best" and the most workable. I have been influenced, obviously, by my training at Ohio University where I worked with both the counselor education and the psychology faculties. They were and are a fine source of encouragement and inspiration and I owe them a great deal.

I am also very much influenced by the ideas of Ernst Beier, Kurt Danzinger, Allen Ivey (who conceived the idea of microcounseling), Jay Haley, Harry S. Sullivan and Carl Rogers. If there is any wisdom to emerge from these pages, it is due to the influence of their concepts.

Without the communication which has occurred between and among my students at Humboldt State University and their willingness to share their ideas, suggestions and reactions with me, this book would probably have never gotten off the "drawing board." I have learned much from them, as well as from those clients with whom I have worked in therapy.

Ms. Linda Weirup, secretary at the Humboldt State Counseling Center, was my typist and managed the impossible feat of bringing clarity out of chaos. I am grateful to her for making the book look like a book. And Carolyn Schrameck, my editor at Carroll Press, is the kind of editor every author should have, providing enthusiastic freedom for me throughout the rewriting process.

Many of the ideas were also "kicked around" with James Knight, my colleague in the psychology department at Humboldt State University. By being obscure, he often forced me into clarity.

The editing and sentence-by-sentence polishing of varying stages of the manuscript are due largely to the efforts of Tracey Barnes

Priestley and Barbara Wallace. Barbara, in particular, made me give up some esoteric phrasing in favor of making sense. The support given by both friends in the face of overwhelming stubbornness on my part is sincerely appreciated.

And finally, I appreciate my son, Christopher, and my daughter, Tai, for being the kind of people who make communication very worthwhile.

PART I: Level One Interactions

1

From Theory to Practice and Back Again

Research in the field of counseling during the last twenty years has presented some interesting findings as well as challenges to the continuing practices of counselor education and training. Contributions to our understanding of the nature of the counseling relationship, the process of interpersonal communication, and the nature of learning have come from many research sources and have changed our view of training. In particular, molecular learning (the learning of small units of behavior) rather than global instruction in behavior has dynamically affected both education and counseling. Instruction in the *theory* (and practice) of counseling and psychotherapy is gradually shifting to instruction in the *practice* (and theory) of counseling and psychotherapy. This reversal of priorities is significant in its effects on training.

For several decades the novice counselor has been set loose, dependent on his/her own resources with a certificate in hand stating that s/he is a bona fide counselor. The novice may not *feel* qualified and may not have a repertoire of behaviors other than those which were modeled or copied from some admired professor at graduate school. Yet the counselor is now "prepared." A counselor-in-training at a major university several years ago might have found situations repeating themselves with an embarrassing frequency, situations where s/he had not the slightest idea what to do. S/he knew, from an adopted behavior theory model, that an appropriate reinforcer was needed for the client, that specific behaviors which were maladaptive were to be "extinguished" and adaptive responses were to be "strengthened." What counselor behaviors are suggested? What exactly does this counselor do to bring the theory to life?

The PROBLEM With THEORY *FIRST*

The counselor-in-training knew, for an adopted client-centered therapy model that s/he was supposed to be warm, accepting and genuine. If unconditional positive regard was communicated to the client, the client would find it easier to trust — probably experience the most significant relationship in his /her life and thereby be able to change. What counselor behaviors are suggested? The directive to "be warm," for example, does not lend itself easily to identifiable behaviors. Does it mean: to smile? To give a friendly hug? To punch someone lightly on the arm? To tell a joke? To wear extra clothing? Or to stand near a heater? With so few definitive guidelines as to the nature and meaning of these global concepts, the only recourse for the counselor-in-training seemed to be straining forward in the chair – trying to *be* the good, attentive, warm, accepting, genuine, caring and curing counselor without the slightest idea how.

The leap then from theory to practice sometimes required a step of the imagination which might boggle the mind and shake the confidence of any counselor-in-training. The translation of practice into theory may be a more attainable goal and a more realistic venture. This venture seems to be a Zeitgeist of psychological thinking in recent years and several influences have contributed to its growth and expansion.

SELF-EXAMINATION Within the FIELD of COUNSELING

Self-examination through evaluation of outcomes of counseling is one of the developments in recent years which has contributed to the shift in training emphasis. There are several antecedents to this development. The work of Eysenck (1952) which scathingly pointed out the lack of significant improvement in clients over control groups which received no therapy challenged almost every professional in the field of counseling and psychotherapy. This criticism of counseling outcome, which was repeated in 1965, has caused a professional self-examination which has in turn spawned a totally new understanding of the counseling process. In 1963 Bergin pointed out that while, in fact, group scores showed no significant improvement, individual scores varied widely in much of the type of research Eysenck was examining. That is, some clients improved and some actually became worse as a result of counseling and psychotherapy, whereas subjects in the control groups who received no counseling stayed pretty much the same. The task then became one of differentiating between those client/therapist combinations wherein the client improved and those combinations wherein the client regressed.

Truax and Carkhuff's (1964, 1967) work on the commonalities across counselor styles and theoretical approaches contributed to an understanding of the differences between effective and ineffective counselors and thus became a second major step in the self-examination sequence. Factors which were found to differentiate between high facilitative (promoting personal growth) counselors and low facilitative (promoting aggravation of client symptoms) could thus be identified and hopefully replicated.

A major step toward replication of specific facilitative behavior came out of the work of Allen and Ryan (1969) and Aubertine (1967), who developed methods of *micro-teaching* — instruction in molecular units of behavior. From its origins in education, Ivey (1971) adapted and expanded the concept for use in the training of counselors. The behaviors which Ivey specified have a not so surprising similarity to many of the characteristics identified by Truax and Carkhuff. Ivey developed the facilitative conditions into specific replicable behaviors, making them more widely accessible to counselor training programs.

A final factor in this trend emerged nationwide during the late 1960's. Federal funding of educational programs had led to congressional and public criticisms of the programs and the budgets which accompanied those programs. *Accountability* reared its head, and public education and school counseling programs may never be the same. The accountability movement stressed specification of behaviors and pressure was strongly applied within the field, on-the-job, and on the practitioner to spell out to his/her supervisors and co-workers what exactly it was that s/he was doing and what benefits accrued to his/her clientele. This clientele extended from the students in the public schools to persons serviced by community agencies to the public at large. Society had decided, perhaps due in part to the flood of "popular" books on psychology and counseling, that it had a right to know what it was getting for its direct or indirect dollar. Self-examination and evaluation blossomed.

The COUNSELING RELATIONSHIP

A second major movement which has assisted in developing a more realistic understanding of the counseling process is significant enough to be listed as a separate topic. There has been considerable focus on the counseling relationship itself during the last twenty years and on variables which foster the strengthening of that relationship. Much of the work on the counseling relationship stems from the client-centered (Rogers, 1951) and existential (May, 1967) theoretical approaches. The emphasis placed by these approaches on the counseling relationship is significant. Both theoretical frameworks postulated that change could not occur unless the relationship existed. Significantly, almost all theoretical approaches now recognize the importance of the relationship to counseling outcome.

Obviously, "relationship" cannot be completely separated from those behaviors which facilitate counseling outcome. In many ways, this overlap is beneficial to the counselor-in-training, because "establishing a relationship" is another one of the theoretical assignments a counselor has. The counselor-in-training frequently has had little understanding of just how to go about carrying out this assignment against impossible yet rather typical odds. The average client who is presented (either by referral or by self) for counseling is usually resistant to counseling, distrustful of others, often hostile, sometimes withdrawn, difficult to like and more than likely unable to sustain intimate contact with others. Yet the counselor has, as his/her charge, the task of "establishing a relationship." And if s/he is unable to do so, s/he may be advised (within his/her theoretical framework) to refer. The counselor who receives this referral has the same difficulties to overcome in establishing a positive, beneficial counselor-client relationship and is probably just as tempted to refer to still another counselor. It is wondered if the beneficial relationships of the not-too-distant past occurred primarily by chance and by a Russian roulette referral game, since there has been a dearth of explicit methodology in the literature for the counselor to use in developing rapport or relationships. Again, the leap from theory to practice requires the stride of a long-distance runner. It is suggested that practice in specific behaviors, which are designed to assist the counselor-in-training in his/her task of establishing relationships can be coordinated with practice in those skills which make a facilitative counselor.

COMMUNICATIONS THEORY

The final source of input into our understanding of the counseling process comes from communications theories. Defining and clarifying the process of communication, in a variety of situations and contexts, has provided an abundance of practical information which aids counselors in understanding the unique form of communciation within the counseling session. Integrating the communications theory with the practice of counseling has been attempted by several practicing counselors and counselor educators (Beier, 1966; Haley, 1967; Ruesch, 1961; Jackson, 1962; Danzinger, 1976; et al.) and much of the emphasis within this book is on understanding communications which occur between counselor and client.

Communications theorists examine several variables which contribute to the process of interpersonal communication. The participants, with their respective mental sets, purposes, attitudes, and personal meanings (vocabulary), the context or setting, the non-verbal cues and the cultural and personal meanings attributed thereto, all influence the message being communicated. The *message* and all it entails has a special meaning throughout this book, and we will be returning to this topic often.

Perhaps it will be useful to summarize a few of the more critical points at this time. We will be examining levels of the message: (1) the obvious content; (2) the emotional investment, connections, meanings and impact; and (3) the latent or private meanings. This examination may appear somewhat arbitrary and artificial to the reader, yet the message can be arbitrarily separated into its content and affective components. These may prove to be considerably more tangible and practical for the counselor-in-training.

There is a substantial basis for viewing the content of the message, or what is actually being communicated, as important. If someone reports that it is hot outside, it is wise to take the message at surface value, without looking for the emotional component or the hidden meanings. Most of our daily communication is on this level — simple exchanges of information — and so it should be. In a world which is fast becoming overcrowded (the majority of people living and working in impacted cities) there is neither time nor inclination for emotional or meaningful exchanges with every personal contact. There are simply too many demands made on individuals during any given day. Buying groceries or purchasing gasoline are informational, surface and often faceless transactions between people. This is appropriate and necessary behavior to maintain some sense of privacy and autonomy in our society. Ironically, it is the very fact that many of us communicate *only* on this level that leaves us feeling faceless and unconnected to others. This, in turn, leads many to seek counseling. And perhaps a way to begin finding connections — relatedness between the speaker and the listener — is through recognition (remembering) what it was that was talked about (content). Our first few activities will be designed to aid the counselor-in-training to attend to *what* is being said, to hear the *content* and to communicate in some way to the speaker that s/he has, in fact, been heard at this basic level of communication. It is a crucial first step for the counselor-in-training. It is not as easy as it may appear since so much emphasis is placed on selective *non*-listening within a culture based on the necessary exchanging of informational, surface communication.

ACTIVITIES

1.   Probably every student enrolls in a counseling program and/or in a counseling technique class with some basic goal, some purpose in mind. The first question that could prudently be asked is *what*. At this point it may be helpful to personalize your reading and ask yourself the following questions:

(a)   What makes a good counselor? Why do I want to be one?

(b)   What kind of counselor do I wish to be? What types of clients will I be working with? In what settings?

(c)   What skills do I have that would assist me in being a good counselor? What personal life experiences have I had that lead me to choose this direction?

(d)   What difficulties might I have? What do I now think I need to learn? What do I want from this course?

The next step is to write some of the thoughts that are generated by these questions into an *informal* communication with the instructor. This paper should be turned in at the next meeting.

2.   Interview a classmate (who will be assigned to you on an alphabetical basis) about why s/he wants to be a counselor. Use a tape recorder to record this interview. Do not worry about skills, quality, format, etc., but do try to listen to what your "client" is saying. Then, talk with another classmate (also as assigned) about why you want to be a counselor. It might be helpful to spend a few moments practicing with the tape recorder before you begin either session. After you have completed both tapes, consider the following questions:

(a)   On which tape (or in which role) did you feel most comfortable? What might be some reasons for this?

(b)   How well did you listen? How well did your counselor listen to you?

(c)   How honest were you on the tape when you were the client? How personal were your statements? What might be some reasons for your being more or less personal and honest?

(d)   How do you feel about the two people you met with during this exercise?

3.   Write down your reactions to these activities and hand them in as feedback to the instructor.

SUGGESTED ADDITIONAL READINGS

Allen, D. and Ryan, K. *Microteaching.* Reading: Addison-Wesley, 1969.

This text explains the concepts of molecular learning. Although directed towards teachers, the premise became the foundation for later development by Ivey and other counselor educators into counseling skills training. It is historically interesting and may generate some research ideas.

Aubertine, H. The use of microteaching in training supervising teachers, in *High School Journal, 51*: 99-106, 1967.

This text is useful for the same reasons as the Allen and Ryan book listed above.

Beier, Ernst G. *The silent language of psychotherapy.* Chicago: Aldine Publishing Co., 1966.

Beier uses considerable communications theory in his view of social learning as a significant influence on behavior disorders and on his conception of the process of therapy. It is a challenging book which examines all of the data that occurs within a counseling session as part of the therapeutic process.

Bergin, Allen E. The effects of psychotherapy: Negative results revisited, *Journal of Counseling Psychology,* 1963, *10*, 244-50.

Bergin's response to Eysenck's article stimulated further research into the problem of differential outcome in therapy. It has become a classic in the literature on outcome of therapy and is strongly recommended for an understanding of the problem.

Danzinger, Kurt. *Interpersonal communication.* New York: Pergamon Press, 1976.

This book is highly recommended as a foundation for many of the basic concepts in this course. Danzinger writes clearly and interestingly about the communication process and its hidden dimensions.

Eysenck, H. J. The effects of psychotherapy: An evaluation, *Journal of Consulting Psychology,* 1952, *16*, 319-324.

Eysenck's original criticisms of therapy outcome, comparing patients who received therapy to those patients who received no therapy and finding no significant differences between the two groups, stimulated much of the outcome therapy research and pushed the counseling profession into a thorough self-evaluation. His findings, which were supported and expanded in the article listed below, still represent one of the strongest challenges to the helping professions.

Eysenck, H. J. The effects of psychotherapy, *International Journal of Psychiatry,* 1965, *1*, 97-144.

Haley, Jay. *Strategies of psychotherapy*. New York: Grune & Stratton, 1967.

Haley, a communications theorist, bridges the gap between the dynamics of interpersonal communication and psychotherapy. His specialty lies in the paradoxes of communication. He believes psychotherapy to be one of the major paradoxes. The text is both interesting and difficult to read.

Ivey, Allen E. *Microcounseling: Innovations in interview training.* Springfield, Illinois: Charles G. Thomas, 1971.

Ivey describes the rationale behind the microcounseling approach to training counselors and includes a hefty amount of research in support of this method's effectiveness.

Jackson, Don D. Interactional psychotherapy, in Morris I. Stein, ed., *Contemporary Psychotherapies*. Glencoe: The Free Press, 1962, pp. 256-271.

Jackson is best noted for his development of the double-bind theory in the etiology and treatment of schizophrenia. However, he has also contributed greatly to the application of communications theory to psychotherapy. This brief, complex article is one of his best.

May, Rollo. *Psychology and the human dilemma*. Princeton: D. Van Nostrand Co., 1967.

Existential theory is traced historically here and its applicability to very human problems is described. This book is also notable for its heavy emphasis on the relationship between client and therapist.

Rogers, Carl. *Client-centered therapy*. Boston: Houghton-Mifflin, 1951.

Although Rogers has modified his theoretical position and his actual counseling style many times since this book was written, it still remains the best source for understanding the essence of the Rogerian approach.

Ruesch, Jurgen. *Therapeutic communication*. New York: W. W. Norton, 1961.

This book is frankly one of my personal favorites for its often brilliant applications of communication principles to therapy. With Beier and Danzinger he is a third author who can strengthen theoretical understanding in the reader.

Scheidel, Thomas M. *Speech communication and human interaction*. Glenview, Illinois: Scott, Foresman & Co., 1972.

For a good basic introduction to the process of interpersonal communication, this text is one of the best available. Many of the major concepts presented in this book are directly applicable to the counseling process.

Truax, C. B. and Carkhuff, R. For better or for worse: The process of psychotherapeutic change, in *Recent advances in behavioral change*. Montreal: McGill University Press, 1964.

This text delineates the variables which seem to differentiate high facilitative counselors from low facilitative counselors which is an important step in understanding and predicting therapeutic outcome. See following source also.

Truax, C. B. and Carkhuff, R. *Toward effective counseling and psychotherapy.* Chicago: Aldine, 1967.

This text is a complete and thorough explanation of the theory developed by Truax and Carkhuff which includes the facilitative conditions which are necessary for positive outcome in therapy. Also included is considerable research into the nature of the conditions.

2

Conversations, Communication and the Interview

There are several situations in which two people sit down with one another and exchange information. The most natural of these situations is a conversation. By implication, at the other end of our hypothetical continuum the counseling situation is an "unnatural act." What may feel natural and comfortable in conversational exchanges may be improper behavior during the counseling interview.

Since most of our interactions with others are conversations, the communications style of the conversational exchange is the one we may be most familiar with, yet that style is generally inappropriate to apply to the counseling interview. In the activities of the last chapter, you conducted an interview — possibly your first. You may have already sensed that it was different in some way from a conversation. It may be helpful at this point to examine the process of communication within a conversation more closely to determine those differences and to understand their significance.

CONVERSATIONS

A logical place to begin considering the phenomenon of counseling seems to be the interaction between two people known as "conversation." From studies of social interaction it has been sensibly observed that there is a pattern to communication in conversations. One person, whom we will designate A, says something to Person B and then waits. It is now Person B's turn to respond. B responds and Person A may then say something further, in which case the conversation proceeds in a very common-sense pattern: A B A B A B A B . . . . . From this interaction we observe that when one person stops talking that action is taken as a cue for the other to begin talking. In a sense, a pause obligates the other party to say something to fill in the silence.

If we compare this pattern to that which occurs in a multi-party group (three or more persons), it is easier to understand the obligatory nature of the two-party communications. The pattern of social communication in three member groups rarely, if ever, occurs in an A B C A B C A B C format. If a pause occurs after Person B's statement, it is equally likely that Person A will speak as Person C. Refraining from participation in the conversation is a generally accepted and recognized privilege in multi-person groups. Person C could refrain from participating in the converation totally and just sit quietly listening during the conversation. Thus, the pattern of speaking in the group could become any variation of the A B C A B C pattern, except perhaps that which is regimented into a strict and unyielding formula. Obviously, in two-party conversation one member cannot refrain from participation or conversation ceases. This learning from *social* interactions frequently is hard to ignore in the counseling setting. Counselors often believe, particularly in the early stages of their training, that whenever a silence occurs in the interview, they should fill that silence. As we shall see in later chapters, what feels *natural* in a silence during a counseling interview is generally inappropriate.

There is another aspect to the two-party conversation which should be considered. The A B A B pattern of communication between two people implies a relationship between the utterance of A and the utterance of B which may or may not exist in reality. Consider the *mis*-communication which occurs in the following:

A: What did you think of the football game?

B: I had a great time, except that it was so cold we just huddled under a blanket.

A: I never saw so many fumbles in my life.

B: Paul picked me up before dinner was even on the table. All I had to eat was a hot dog.

A: Did you see the one Evans made?

B: . . . . . the hot dog?

A: No . . . . . the fumble!

In the above example, the two participants are having a conversation. They can be said to be talking *to* each other, though not necessarily communicating. Let us consider another example:

A: Hi, how are you?

B: Have a rotten headache.

A: That's good. See you later.

And another:

A: What are we having for dinner tonight?

B: Chicken. I wish you'd talk to Junior about his room.

A: I wish we'd have that pot roast again.

B: I told him this morning about that room and he still hasn't cleaned it.

A: Martin took that sales contract right out from under my nose today.

B: Anyway, I wish you'd talk to Junior. He listens to you.

All three of these examples are very common occurrences in social conversation. In each example both participants observe the social amenities of communication: They take turns, interruptions are held to a minimum and each is apparently hearing the other in one sense. That is, Person B is obviously aware when Person A has stopped talking. Otherwise, how would Person B know when to begin? The hypothesis that is suggested here is that there is more to communication than verbalization and waiting for your turn to produce more verbalization. Speier (1973), who has studied the patterns of social communication extensively, states, "A conversation consists as much of the phenomenon of hearing as it does of speaking." It is the definition and varied interpretations of "hearing" which cause difficulties in communication. What Person A says in the conversation is one thing; what Person B *hears* is something else. Hearing may begin as simple awareness that Person A has started talking and at some point stops talking, allowing and even obligating Person B to respond. The range of hearing may include recognition of simple word meanings (comprehension) and/or awareness of shared meanings between the participants (codes) as Altman and Taylor (1973) point out in their study of the communication process. Hearing may also include recognition of words which have unique meanings to the speaker as well as recognition of words which could be misunderstood. Most social listening stops just short of comprehension. To look for deeper meanings in social exchanges is usually inappropriate. In social conversations going beyond what is said, interpreting the hidden meaning behind the content of what is expressed is usually unnecessary, time-consuming and frequently violates existing social mores about respecting the privacy of friends and social acquaintances. Again, the type and quality of listening which is "natural" in conversations is very different from that required in a counseling interview. Unfortunately, social learning has limited the listening abilities of most people — including those who would be counselors.

Listening in Social Conversation

Boy (1974) points out that most Americans have limited listening abilities; that is, they listen with judgmental ears, waiting for the speaker to pause so that they can agree or disagree with his/her statement.   Frequently, the listener is using judgmental listening to select potential friends and associates. The listener can categorize the statements made by the speaker into those which are in agreement or disagreement with the listener's value system. If the statements are in agreement, the speaker has the potential of being a friend, and at the least, is certainly considered more interesting and wise than if the statements are in disagreement or conflict with the values of the listener. Thus listening frequently becomes a tool for determining attraction: The speaker is interesting and/or agrees with the listener's views; for determining distance: The speaker is boring and/or disagrees with the listener's views. Since quite a few of the social relationships in the listener's lifetime are formed in just this manner, the sensitivities required for effective listening are often short-circuited by evaluative judgments. This natural tendency to evaluate as we listen in social conversations is inappropriate in the counseling interview.

Other factors contribute to limited listening abilities. One, which may be apparent from the length of the current discussion, has to do with energy. Listening requires an energy expenditure. A remarkable parallel is provided by the action of studying a fairly difficult reading passage. Studying requires focusing of attention on the passage and away from distracting events. The student may also return consciously again and again to the passage after "mind detours" and recognition of internal stimuli, such as a stomach growling in hunger. Each return of attention requires an additional energy expenditure. Obviously, a related problem is the amount of external and internal distractions. The listener, like the student, must concentrate on what is being said and return his/her attention back to the speaker after each distraction. All of this requires energy.

A related difficulty which blocks effective listening is a kind of emotional distraction occurring within the listener. If words uttered by the speaker serve as stimuli for emotional reactions and mental images within the listener, concentration is broken and energy is again required to return to attention. Words which frequently stimulate "mind detours" or serve as cues for emotional reactions for counselors-in-training are: death, sex, Christian, Jew, Democrat, abortion, drunk, drugs and Robert Redford. Actually, the list is seemingly endless and varies from listener to listener, but perhaps the sampling listed in this paragraph is enough to clarify the difficulty.

Words also have varied content meanings. Words emitted by the speaker frequently have one meaning for the speaker and a totally different one for the listener. This can lead to problems which range from simple misunderstandings of homonyms (e. g., week for weak) to varying meanings for the same word (such as fumble in the conversation described earlier) to different understandings of words based on ethnic or regional backgrounds.

In summary, several factors contribute to ineffective listening: first, the conversational style of listening which has been socially learned by all of us; second, judgmental listening which is considering the content of what is being said in terms of agreement or disagreement; third, the availability of the necessary energy to focus attention away from internal and external stimuli and back to the speaker; fourth, simple understanding of the language used; fifth, internal emotional responses to what is being said; and sixth, the assumption of incorrect meanings and/or emotional meanings in the speaker by the listener. Undoubtedly, there are other factors which interfere. Those which have been discussed in the preceding pages may serve as a reminder of the quality of listening which is acceptable in conversations and social situations and unacceptable in counseling.

Effective listening is basic to the counseling process and is a necessary preliminary to conditions which would foster growth and change. Obviously, it is also a necessary preliminary to any of the behavioral units which are classifed as counseling skills.

The INTERVIEW as an EXCHANGE of INFORMATION

Aside from conversations there are several settings in which two people exchange information. What makes this action an interview or a counseling session has been the subject of considerable theorizing and investigation. Several writers in the behavioral sciences do not differentiate between counseling and interviewing. For those writers the position is taken that the interview is basic to the counseling function; that one comes before the other, or that each individual counseling session is called an interview. Benjamin (1969) differentiates the interview into two types. In the first type, the client (interviewee) helps the counselor (interviewer) by giving information. The counselor, however, determines just what type of help s/he obtains from the client by the form and wording of the questions. Examples of this type are: the television interview, the journalistic interview, the job interview wherein the information obtained is used to make a decision about the client, and the intake interview used by many institutional organizations in an attempt to determine the best possible placement for the client. In some ways control of the client's time and behavior is implicit in this type of interview. The welfare worker needs to focus on the income problems of the welfare recipient; other kinds of information are not pertinent in the interview. Similarly, the physician needs to obtain information about other areas of the patient's life. In both examples, the "counselor" is gathering information in order to make decisions about the life changes of the client. The type of information sought is directly related to the purpose of the interview and thereby under the control and discretion of the "counselor."

A training program designed to prepare interviewers of this type should have as its focus training in the kinds of skills which are necessary to elicit the most meaningful information in the shortest possible time. The interviewer's primary concern would be how to stay on pre-selected topics long enough to elicit just the required amount of information. Economy would be stressed; time-consuming digressions would be avoided. For the purposes of this course, this type of interview is differentiated from counseling even though information obtained in this manner could be helpful to counselors. The interview as *obtaining information* is not the goal of this course.

The COUNSELING INTERVIEW

Benjamin's second type of interview has, at least as an implied goal, the purpose of helping the *client*, rather than the purpose of obtaining information. There may be some side benefits for the counselor in this type of interview: Information is given (rather than obtained), the counselor may feel useful or needed or somewhat omnipotent, and perhaps the counselor makes a living. The real payoffs of the interaction between counselor and client in this type of interview are intended for the client. The counselor keeps the client as the focus of the interview (rather than focusing on information that the counselor wishes to discuss or obtain) and within the session gives control in many ways to the client. There is an interesting rationale for this action. The ultimate goal of shifting the control within the session is to aid the client in taking control of other areas of his/her life as well. Additional ways of facilitating this response in the client will be discussed in a later section of this book. The consistency of this goal with the behavior of the counselor in this type of interview is obvious. The counselor allows more freedom for digressions, discussing topics which are pertinent to the client, and allowing the client to determine the direction of the conversation. This action is particularly noticeable in the earlier stages of the counseling relationship.

The focus of this book is on training counselors who can conduct counseling interviews of this type. The counselor has to be able to keep the client as the focus of the interview. The counselor has to be able to put aside any informational goals in favor of the topic the client is discussing, and s/he has to be able to follow, rather than lead, the discussion. A training program generated by this type of interview is considerably different from the training program generated by an information-obtaining interview. The skills required are more complex and have more of an interpersonal focus. Yet the primary skill of listening is still the basic unit upon which all other counseling skills rest.

Listening in the Counseling Interview

Ivey (1971) suggests that there are behavioral components of listening which can be described, practiced and learned. Perhaps the perfection of any skill requires a conscious application of the molecular units or specific behaviors within that skill. In practicing a new musical piece on any instrument, the recommended procedure, and the one which would provide the best results for the learner, is to hear the piece being played, to practice each unit (e. g., the fingering on a difficult passage) until mastered as a unit, and then put it together as a total performance. The analogy from music can be directly applied to counseling behaviors. Ivey recommends the same method in learning how to listen. His concept of attending behavior (listening) is basic to all other skills in his microcounseling training program sequence. And, as a matter of fact, attending behavior seems to be the one skill which is basic to all counseling styles and across many theoretical approaches. Since we have found that our social training and our conversational skills are *not* conducive to good listening patterns within the counseling interview, we will begin with the behavioral components of attentive listening.

There are three basic components which have been identified as characteristics of attentive listeners: (a) posture, (b) eye contact, and (c) verbal following.

The posture of the counselor should appear natural and relaxed. The physical comfort of the counselor will do much to minimize internal bodily distractions. Slouching in a chair, while not particularly recommended as an appropriate counselor position, is certainly preferred over a stiff and upright manner. Using an observer, the counselor-in-training might try several sitting positions in different chairs until s/he finds those positions which both feel comfortable and appear comfortable to the observer. Body position can be turned toward the client, with a one and one-half to four foot space between the counselor and the client. This distance, while seeming arbitrary, seems to coincide well with what Hall (1966) describes as "personal distance." This is defined as "a small protective sphere or bubble that an organizm maintains between itself and others." Personal distance is a function of the closeness of a relationship. A reduction of the physical space to less than eighteen inches represents a mutual recognition of a differing, closer degree of intimacy. The counseling relationship, while varying in intimacy, would be wise to respect that personal distance space of the client.

Bodily position in relationship to the client has also been examined rather specifically. Facing the client directly apparently causes some uneasiness, and at early stages in the counseling relationship the goal should be to reduce threat and tension rather than to increase it. Placing two chairs in a curved line or at an oblique angle (with or without a table between them) has been recommended to increase ease and comfort in the participants.

Eye contact refers to looking at the client while s/he is talking. It does not mean staring, however. Since many persons are uncomfortable with prolonged eye contact and since client-initiated eye contact tends to decrease during anxiety-provoking discussions, the counselor should take his/her cue from the client. If the client is avoiding eye contact it would seem to be fruitless for the counselor to continue trying to catch the client's eyes. Looking at the client without intensity and not staring indicates that you are interested in what the client has to say. An interesting finding from research may have some implications for the counselor-in-training. It seems that when the client pauses, looks at the counselor and waits for a response from the counselor, the beginning counselor tends to look away before responding. At that point in the counseling session the beginning counselor may need to expend additional energy in order not to break the client-initiated eye contact. In summary, eye contact should be used with discretion. If the client gives cues that s/he is uncomfortable, eye contact should be reduced. If, on the other hand, the client initiates eye contact, the counselor should respond in kind.

The third component of attending behavior is "the interviewer's use of comments which follows directly from what the interviewee is saying" (Ivey, 1971). Verbal following is perhaps the most difficult of the three behavioral components and the one which will feel the most awkward to practice. Allowing the client to speak without interruption, following what is being said by asking related questions and making comments about the topic without changing the subject are not really typical modes of social interaction. The insertion of personal views, agreeing or disagreeing about the subject, is inappropriate in attending behavior. The task of the counselor is to listen and to make his/her presence known as a *listener*, not as a speaker. The resemblance to a conversation should be decreasing noticeably at this point.

ACTIVITIES

1.   Listen to a conversation between two people (either live or televised). Using a small sample of the conversation (five minutes) make notes on what you hear. Note the topic discussed. Did it change? Who initiated changes of topic? Are the two participants listening to one another? How close are they to one another physically? Does this change? How can you tell if they are listening to each other? Do they acknowledge what each other is saying? Are they looking at one another? How much eye contact do they have?

2.   In small groups practice carrying on a conversation of an introductory nature while standing back to back. Repeat the exercise using personal distance and repeat again using intimate distance (less than eighteen inches). Are there differences in the three situations? How did they feel?

3.   Have someone in your group read one or two short paragraphs to you while in a counseling seating arrangement. At the end of each paragraph, relate what you heard. Have others in your group check you on your listening accuracy. What stimuli were you aware of as distractions?

4.   Sit quietly with someone in a counseling seating arrangement for two or three minutes. Do not talk. Maintain eye contact that is *comfortable* for the two of you. Do not stare. What did you think about? How comfortable were you?

5.   Make a practice interview tape using the behavioral components of listening. Select a member of your group to be your "client." Discuss a problem your "client" had while s/he was in high school. Do not worry about how the problem was solved or whether the problem was resolved. Restrict the discussion to the "client's" topic and the situation assigned. The time limit on this tape is five to seven minutes. Repeat the taping experience with another member of your group with yourself in the role of client. How did you feel during each of the two experiences? Were you aware of attending behaviors in yourself as counselor? — in your partner while you were the client? Complete an evaluation sheet for your counselor and share the comments with him/her. Were you able to be honest with your comments or did you feel pressure to be "nice?" Was the evaluation from your client helpful to you? What would you do differently on your next tape?

6.   Write down your reactions to these activities (feedback) and give these comments to the instructor.

SUGGESTED ADDITIONAL READINGS

Altman, I. and Taylor, D. *Social penetration: The development of interpersonal relationships*. New York: Holt, Rinehart and Winston, 1973.

This text is an interesting though complex discussion of the factors which contribute to the development of interpersonal relationships. A description of communication in social settings includes a discussion of codes, shared meanings, mis-communication and understandings which should prove helpful to the counselor who is interested in further understanding the process of communication.

Benjamin, Alfred. *The helping interview*. Boston: Houghton-Mifflin, 1969.

Benjamin gives many practical suggestions to the counselor-in-training about seating arrangements, beginning an interview and determining the purposes of the interview. His differentiation of the counseling interview into two types, the information-obtaining interview and the helping interview helps to clarify counselor goals in approaching the interview. This is an excellent source book.

Boy, Angelo V. Clients in the school, in *The counselor's handbook*, Gail F. Farwell, *et al.*, editors. New York: Intext Educational Publishers, 1974.

This article is particularly pertinent for its discussion of social listening, evaluative listening and the differing quality of listening required from the counselor.

Fast, Julian. *Body language*. New York: M. Evans & Co., 1970.

Fast describes the many messages which are communicated nonverbally in the American culture. Of particular interest to counselors is his description of the cultural implications of eye contact and staring.

Fenlason, Anne F. *Essentials in interviewing*. New York: Harper and Row, 1962.

Intended for social workers, the primary focus of this book is on the information-obtaining interview and the economics of pursuing relevant topics in short periods of time. There is a good section on developing trust in the relationship.

Gottman, John M. and Leiblum, Sandra R. *How to do psychotherapy and how to evaluate it*. New York: Holt, Rinehart and Winston, 1974.

This interesting book makes extensive use of a flow-chart conceptualization of counseling. The counselor is trained to be a self-correcting organism — at any step in the counseling process s/he can check his/her own progress. If the process is continuing in a productive direction, the counselor goes on to the next step in the sequence. If not, the counselor can retrace his/her steps and correct. This book is helpful in determining listening behaviors.

Hall, E. T. *The hidden dimension*. Garden City: Doubleday, 1966.

In this book Hall introduces his now classic concepts of social distance, personal distance and intimate distance. Their usefulness to the understanding of personal space in counseling and in interpersonal relationships is considerable and worthy of further attention.

Ivey, Allen E. *Microcounseling: Innovations in interview training.* Springfield: Charles C. Thomas, 1971.

Ivey describes the rationale behind the microcounseling approach to training counselors and includes a hefty amount of research in support of this method's effectiveness. Specific directions for each of the skills are included.

Klas, L. and Peters, Herman J. Counseling interview techniques: A comparison of theory and practice, *Counselor Education and Supervision*, 1973, *13*, 137-143.

The authors list some sixty different counseling techniques and indicate the techniques which seem to be common across counseling theories and styles. Considerable support is given to the primary skill of attentive listening.

Speier, Matthew. *How to observe face-to-face communication: A sociological introduction.* Pacific Palisades: Goodyear Publishing Co., 1973.

Intending to assist behavioral science students engaged in natural research and observation, Speier points out differences between two-party communication (and its obligatory nature) and multi-party communication. The process of communication in social settings is clearly described. Drawings and graphs are included which aid in understanding Speier's conceptualizations.

3

Skill Acquisition and Content Responses

The VALUE of SKILL ACQUISITION

The recent trend in counselor education has been away from global learning and toward molecular learning. Actually, what passed for global learning in the not-too-distant past, was a strong emphasis on theory in the trainee's educational program. Counselor training in many universities during the 60's studiously avoided any direct teaching of skills, under the assumption that counselors would find their own way of experience. A heavy grounding in theory was supposed to "suggest" the appropriate techniques. While knowledge of a theoretical framework is indispensable to the practicing counselor, the jump from theory to practice was assumed, not taught. When the student had developed a theoretical position — or a strong understanding and acceptance of an existing theoretical position — s/he then was exposed to direct experience, either within the protected on-campus practicum environment or on the job. At that point, through correction and feedback by a supervisor of what the student counselor was doing *within his/her theoretical framework*, s/he developed skills.

The global method is inefficient for several reasons. First, translating a theoretical approach into specific behaviors is a leap which is somewhat analogous to falling into water and knowing that if you do "it" right you'll stay afloat. Second, the specific behaviors which the trainee learned were often far more dependent on what kinds of clients s/he was exposed to and what skills the supervisor had found useful in that situation than the theoretical approach itself. Finally, and perhaps most importantly, this method tended to perpetuate given theoretical approaches, *without* incorporating the considerable data researchers were finding as to the techniques which seemed to be most effective across theoretical positions. Researchers were beginning to answer the questions of *what* happens in a counseling interview and *what* is effective.

This led to a definition and labelling of specific counseling behaviors. Some of these were extremely specific, such as eye contact and bodily position. Others were more complex, such as listening (which *also* can be broken down into specific component behaviors — such as bodily position and eye contact!). Throughout this book, the attempt is made to move from the simple to the complex, and to examine each skill through its molecular (smaller) components.

   A.   Accountability.   One distinct value of skill acquisition, with its concomitant abilities to define and label the skills utilized as well as their purpose in the interview, is suggested to counselors by an interesting word called "accountability." With increasing federal support of mental health programs in schools and the community, there is a related tendency to evaluate results. In fact, it is generally a requirement. This strong trend toward accountability in the counseling interview mandates the ability to specify *what* happens and *what is* effective. The emphasis on specific behavioral skills is consistent with the current emphasis on accountability. Counseling skills can be directly observed, described and measured in a way theory cannot. The need for counselors to know *what* they are doing, to validate and self-correct their own procedures is mandatory in the current climate of accountability.

   Thus, the value of skill acquisitions stems from our research findings, is enhanced by understanding the purposes of the skills to be learned and is consistent with accountability.

   B.   Memorization vs. Understanding Behavior.   There seems to be a definite advantage in understanding the final purpose of the skill to be learned in the molecular acquisition of behaviors. For the student of any subject, straight memorization of skills has been found to be rather ineffective, yet when the purpose or potential value and usefulness of the skill is incorporated into the training program, skill development proceeds at a faster rate and the skills are retained longer.

   The value of techniques *per se* is becoming increasingly recognized. Robinson (1950) was one of the first counselor educators to recognize and describe a taxonomy of counseling leads. Frequently psychologists will look upon techniques with disdain, assuming even now that if the counselor-in-training has a thorough grounding in a theoretical approach, an understanding of the communication process and a sincere desire to "help" people, techniques will magically become obvious and available to him/her. Again, a heavy grounding in theory was supposed to "suggest" the appropriate techniques. As London points out: "This is not so, of course, since the same theory may suggest several techniques and a single technique be deduced from many theories." There also seems to be a tendency to view particular techniques as narrowly affiliated with particular theoretical approaches. Imagine the embarrassment of a behaviorist who finds the techniques s/he is using re-define him/her as a client-centered therapist (London, 1964).

"Embarrassment is both unfortunate and unnecessary" in London's view, however. "The analysis of techniques serves understanding more than any other possible approach to this dicipline, mainly because techniques are relatively concrete things, and to that extent are not only simpler to describe accurately than theories or philosophies but also more relevant indices of what actually goes on in therapy" (London, 1964).

The advantages of a consideration of techniques and responses are several. One, they can be taught directly, in a way that theory cannot, and remain separate from theory. As Ivey points out: "To generate alternative behaviors, one must have a background of skills from which one can draw" (Ivey, 1971). Thus, a counselor with many alternative behaviors can select the most appropriate for his/her intent and style within the counseling session.

A related advantage has to do with the specificity of techniques. It is possible to examine what a technique is and does, then to consider how it fits into the larger system of the interview and, finally, to consider the why of counseling behaviors and how growth is promoted by those behaviors. We are proceeding from molecular to molar considerations of behavior. The complexity of modern life has resulted in a complexity of emotional problems. What follows this is a need for examining and upgrading the specialized skills which attempt to cope with those problems in a counseling interview. Each counselor is responsible for developing the widest repertoire of abilities so that s/he in turn is able to select appropriately for the particular counseling relationship under focus (Farwell, 1974). "Counselors lose much of their effectiveness without a sufficiently deep and broad repertoire of counseling interview techniques" (Klas and Peters, 1973).

An additional question could be reasonably asked at this point. Does training in the techniques of counselor responses make a difference? Research cited by Ivey (1971) and others indicates that it does. Knowing that these skills make a difference and knowing the purpose and potential value of the target skill can help overcome the resistance the student often feels to the drill involved in the task of practicing.

C. *Artificiality and Reality.* As Ivey(1971) points out, practicing the attending behavior skills may seem somewhat artificial to counselors-in-training. They validly object to viewing counseling as a "handbag" of tricks or skills which the counselor dips into during the

interview. The seeming artificiality of practicing a specific behavior
may grossly interfere with a counselor's desire to be "real" and "honest." Perhaps an analogy could be made here to a beginning tennis
player. Before someone plays a match, s/he must acquire some skills:
s/he needs to know how to balance his/her weight on the balls of his/
her feet, how to address the ball, how to grip the racquet correctly,
how to use the wrist, how to follow through and how to place the
ball so that s/he does not expend all his energy running all over the
court. The example could be expanded but perhaps the point has
been made. A skilled tennis player no longer *thinks* those movements during the game (unless the player becomes aware during the
game that s/he is getting sloppy with footwork or wrist action) but
plays with the "honest" and "real" conviction of winning the match
or gaining some exercise. Even practicing becomes real to the serious
tennis player. Practice can also become real to the serious counselor.

Reality is augmented due to the interaction between client and
counselor. Initially, the counselor's efforts to focus on posture, eye
contact and verbal following may be stilted and awkward. Yet the
reinforcing nature of attending behaviors has an effect on the client.
The client, sensing s/he is being listened to, continues to elaborate
his/her topic and develops some enthusiasm in the interview. As Ivey
points out, this in turn reinforces the counselor and it becomes not
only much easier to continue listening but much more real. Feelings
of inadequacy to the task, feelings of awkwardness and self-con-
sciousness may frequently occur in learning new counseling skills.
Those feelings as well as others which occur in the counseling session in *both* participants are real. Unfortunately, the tendency then
is to deflect those feelings into a rationale of artificiality. The
emphasis on skill acquisition often feels negating to the counselor as
a person.

The description and listing of counselor responses is not intended to oversimplify the process of counseling or the importance
of the counselor-as-person. Memorization of a large variety and number of responses will *not* provide the counselor with the magical gift
of being able to counsel. There is no intent to oversimplify, as the
use of techniques does not in itself constitute counseling. If techniques were equatable with counseling, perhaps a feedback-type of
machine could serve the counselor function. The counselor, in addition to a wide knowledge of techniques, brings an individual
"intent" or purpose, theoretical framework, empathy, caring and
the dynamics of the relationship itself to the counseling session. A
counselor is more than a set of learned responses, just as a song is
more than a series of notes. Sharing knowledge of techniques is
only one way of sharing skill as a counselor and as a person

COMMUNICATION – Level One

Once the counselor begins considering verbal responses which will serve a purpose in the interview, s/he begins to approach several communicative processes and levels simultaneously. One, the counselor must be concerned about the selection of the response, although for the trained and experienced counselor this apparently occurs without too much deliberation. Secondly, the purpose of the response must be considered – what s/he wants the response to *do* in the counseling interview. Thirdly, the counselor must be aware of the level of communication as it exists in that moment and whether the response will change the level of communication.

At the first level of communication, it is hypothesized that content is being expressed.

In the following pages several counseling responses will be described. Most of them are described in terms of purpose – what they tend to do with the counseling session. Almost all of them are "content" responses – that is, they address themselves to the content of what is being said and do not change the level of communication. Level One of our tentative framework is the content level and is characterized by content responses from the counselor.

Content responses aid the prospective counselor in developing listening accuracy. The counselor does not need to be concerned with changing client perceptions, with exploring the realm of feelings behind the content – only with being relatively certain s/he understands what is being said. The counselor is truly a non-judgmental listener at this point. The counselor seeks to know the meaning of the experience, seeks to remember it without distortions or omissions so that, at a later point in the counseling relationship it can be "put together" in some meaningful framework with the client.

At this communication level, the counselor is not focusing on the feelings behind the words themselves. This is frequently a wise course of action, for there is often a too rapid jump into the realm of emotions before the counselor and client have an adequate picture of the reality of the situation or have developed a relationship. Finally, the responses vary widely in the effects they have upon the counseling relationship. For the most part, the reponses described herein have a positive effect. The majority of them provide steady, if small, doses of support and encouragement to the counseling relationship.

A. *Content Responses.* As our skill-building is additive, it may be helpful to review at this point the listening skills (attending behavior) developed in your first taping session and any problems encountered in their mastery.

Bodily posture and eye contact are usually relatively simple skills to master. Verbal following, the third behavioral component of attending behavior, seems somewhat more difficult to acquire. Trouble spots seem to occur in the use of questions which shift the focus either slightly or sharply away from the client's expressed content. Selecting phrases which were used by the client to restate what has been said will expand the content. The counselor should not assume the responsibility for expanding the discussion. Asking oneself the question, "Am I adding new information to the discussion?" will generally assist the counselor to avoid asking questions which shift the focus.

The use and misuse of questions is a special consideration for the counselor in training. Frequently beginning counselors utilize questions in an attempt to control the interview situation. Unsure of themselves and their ability to counsel, they seek information and sometimes set up a "chaining" pattern of question and answer which is very hard to break. In effect, the client is introduced to the counseling situation by questions and begins to expect that the responsibility for the session time lies in the hands of the counselor. The counselor will ask questions, the client will provide the answers. The client may assume that this is the only way the counselor has of helping him/her (Benjamin, 1969).

Historically, the beginning counselor has a great deal of precedent for the use of questions. In previous considerations of the scientific study of neuroses and maladjustments, much emphasis was placed upon the motivation of behavior. In psychoanalytic therapies, if the patient understood the motivation for his/her behavior the patient then would be able to experience relief from his/her symptoms, if not bring the behavior under control. If the client was not able to determine the why of his/her behavior, it was a therapist's function to determine it for the client. What seems surprisingly apparent in this is that most clients have no idea why they behave in the way they do — call it unconscious motivations, distorted perceptions or confusion — but if clients could explain why they did the things they did (and why they felt they way they felt) they very likely wouldn't seek counseling in the first place. To ask the client the why of anything usually results in defensiveness rather than answers. When a client is asked why s/he did something it also leads to rationalization of behavior and does not increase understanding or change. The defensive feelings are quite real, as any interrogated adolescent coming home late will avow.

In modern psychology the emphasis is not on the why, but the how or what. Support for this shift comes from both the behaviorists and the communication theorists. "The modern operationalist is more interested in observing the impact which behavior produces upon itself, others, and the material world than in speculating about hypothetical causes . . . communication theory . . . explains the repetitiveness of certain behavioral acts by the absense of negative feedback and the presence of positive feedback which maximizes a certain kind of behavior" (Ruesch, 1961). One communications theorist (Haley, 1963) goes so far as to stop his clients when they begin explaining their behavior, informing them that his task is to work with the "what."

There are, of course, certain places in an interview where the use of questions, other than whys, is appropriate. Yet, as an option among many available to the counselor it is not the strongest or most effective choice.

There is a large difference between the following:

"How does the new job seem to you?"

"I wonder how the new job seems to you."

The former is a direct question and requires a direct answer. The latter, while still an inquiry, is indirect and is more open in its response options than the former. It leaves the greater bulk of the responsibility of the direction of the interview in the hands of the client.

Alternatives to questions should be used whenever possible, and the following types of questions should be avoided at all costs.

→*Closed questions* are those which can be answered by a one-word response, yes, no, or specific informational words. This type of question does not expand the topic but closes it, leaving it up to the counselor to ask another question in order to continue the conversation.

Example: Are you enjoying school?

→*Double-barrelled questions* are those which have two choices paired in the same inquiry. They have the same hazards built-in as closed questions, with the added disability of limiting to two choices rather than expanding the options available to the client.

Example: Would you rather be in school or working on a job?

→*Multiple-choice questions* tend to occur in verbose counselors who tend to try to specify all the options available and pin the client down to the selection of one. Not only are they limiting but they are confusing to the client.

Example: Did you get angry when your mom told you that you couldn't go to the party or did you understand her decision or did you just feel badly?

→*Leading questions* imply that the answer is already known to the counselor. As such, they are extremely limiting and highly directive. Many clients find it difficult to disagree or veer away from the implied expected response.

Example: You didn't really mean to do this, did you?

Example: Did anyone put a gun to your head and force you to drop out of school?

→*Probing questions* are probably best described by comparing them to the kinds of questions frequently asked by the stereotyped caricature of the nosy neighbor. The questions often cause embarrassment and discomfort. In the counseling interview such questions are embarrassing to the client, very directive as to topic and inappropriately shift the content level to another level entirely, just because of the feelings aroused. Probes often shift the topic also.

Example: Was there another woman involved in your decision to get a divorce?

Example: Does anyone else in your family have sexual problems?

The only questions which can be used, and then very sparingly, are open-ended questions. Open-ended questions are phrased so that the client can make a wide array of responses and answer with more than one or two words. They do not limit or suggest the kind of response anticipated by the counselor. These kinds of questions are called general leads.

1. *General Leads.* These responses include broad invitations to the client to provide more information on the logical content or a related issue. They are *not* forcing maneuvers by the counselor to direct the interview or to probe into uncharted waters before the client has expressed willingness to discuss topics. These leads generally help to clarify the communicative processes occuring during a session.

Example: Client: The doctor is really hypocritical. It seems as if all he wants to do is give me medication and I just can't fight him.

Counselor: Could you tell me more about this?
                              or
              Would you give me an example of what you mean by hypocritical?

Purpose: Here the counselor is asking for expansion.

Example: Counselor: How have things been going this week?

Purpose: Often used as an opening lead at the beginning of the interview.

Example: Counselor: What would you like to talk about today?

Purpose: Often used as an opening lead at the beginning of the interview.

Example: Counselor: (after long verbalization followed by long silence) Where are we?

Purpose: Here the counselor is expressing confusion as to the direction of the interview and inviting clarification by the client.

2. *Minimal Encourages.* Under the category of minimal encourages are all of these verbalizations which are first of all designed to indicate acceptance of the client, interest in what is being said (reinforcement of content), and a wish not to interrupt. They are designed to assist the client in continuing to talk. When used correctly, minimal encourages free the counselor from the search for a "vital" or meaningful response to the client and simply indicate the counselor's wish for the client to continue. Beginning with Greenspoon's research in 1955, psychologists have taken a special interest in the use of counselor acceptance as exemplified by minimal encourages and nodding as reinforcers. One can deny the potency of these behaviors and all other responses of the counselor as reinforcers or one can acknowledge their effectiveness and use them in a discriminating manner. The latter course of action is strongly recommended. It is interesting to note Truax's examination of counseling comments by Carl Rogers during therapy (1966). Truax concluded that Rogers was differentially reinforcing his clients by applying and withholding his attention and verbalization, particularly including responses of the minimally encouraging type. It appears that counselor's verbal responses are one category of the behavior influencing processes involved in counseling and therapy (Dustin & George, 1973). Problems which beginning counselors usually encounter in the use of minimal encourages are in their overuse or in using them as fillers for every pause or natural break in the speaker's train of thought. A good guideline may come from the client; if the client is ending sentences or phrases with an inflection and looking at the counselor as if to check if the counselor is still "with" him, those seem to be appropriate times for minimal encourages.

Example: Client: I don't seem to have the energy to get up in the mornings.

Counselor: Mmm-hmmm.

Purpose: A continuing or encouraging response to indicate that the counselor would like to hear more
about this problem.

3. *Silence.* By far the most underused of the content responses, this response frequently indicates to the client that we can wait for the client to finish his/her thought, to find the elusive words, and to clarify his/her own thinking. Consider the A B A B A B pattern of conversation discussed in Chapter Two. When A stops, it is usually a cue for B to make a comment. If B does not, then A will frequently assume B thinks s/he is not finished and will either continue to talk or will reflect for a moment on what has just been said. Again, eye contact is a good clue as to the correct recourse. If the client is staring expectantly and fixedly at the counselor, the counselor might attempt another type of response to indicate s/he is still with the client. If the client is thinking or looking like s/he is pondering the meaning of what has just been said, then it is probably ill-advised to insert an expectant "mmm-hmmm." A better course of action is to wait.

Thus the silence is frequently considered to be an alternative to the use of minimal encourages. Paul (1973) describes silence as listening impassively and prefers to listen rather than minimally encourage for one basic reason. "The fundamental advantage is that it avoids exerting control over what your patient communicates; at the very least, it keeps such control at a minimum . . . for instance, if you say "I see" or "uh-huh" when s/he has uttered a statement about his/her feelings, this will reinforce such statements – and we know such reinforcements can be effective in increasing the rate of such statements. In this way, the simplest of signals and gestures can exert a significant control over the patient's verbalization, and that is what we must avoid or at least minimize. By now it should be clear to you how basic it is . . . that the patient experience, if not enjoy, freedom to say what s/he will" (Paul, 1973).

Example: Client: I couldn't believe she would react like
that.
        Counselor: . . . . .

        Purpose: By the use of silence here, the counselor is in-
viting the client to expand on how "she" re-
acted, what reaction had been expected and
how the client felt.

4. *Restatement.* Restatements serve the purpose of continuing the flow of the client's remarks and encouraging him/her to expand. As well, they indicate close listening behavior to the client. Restatements utilize the exact vocabulary of the client and may consist of one word, a phrase or a sentence. As such, restatements are frequently

referred to as mirroring or echo responses. They are not meaningless echoes, however. Their directive reinforcing content is a function of the selectiveness of restatement choices by the counselor and is demonstrated in the second example below. Restatements are "immediate" responses in that the response is matched in every way to the characteristics of the client's initial statement (Ruesch, 1961). Obviously inflection should match the client's. The usual reaction to restatement by counselors-in-training is discomfort with their awkwardness. This awkwardness is demonstrated by over-inflection of the selected word or phrase. When a client uses the briefest of phrases to describe his/her experiences, the counselor by selective use of restatements can assist the client in expanding and clarifying the experiences. The conversation is not a real conversation at all in that the pattern of communication here should look something like A B A B A B, with the contributions of B intended to be part of the flow of and mirroring A:

Example: Client: I haven't been able to sleep for a week.

Counselor: You're not able to sleep.

Purpose: A simple restatement of the "gist" of the client's statement.

Example: Client: I went to an interview. There were so many people there that I was discouraged, and I went and bought a cup of coffee instead of waiting.

Counselor: You bought a cup of coffee.

Purpose: The directive reinforcement of the choice of the coffee statement to restate is shown here (rather than the discouragement or not waiting). The choice could lead the interview into a whole new area, i. e., what happened at the coffee shop.

ACTIVITIES

1. Read the following transcript of a counseling interview described by Benjamin (1969) wherein questions are used a great deal. Imagine yourself in the role of client. What would you be feeling at the four reaction points indicated on the transcript?

Counselor: Hello, Jack, come right in. I'm the placement officer at the center. I understand you'll be leaving us soon. What would you like to do when you get out?

Client: I don't know exactly. You see. . .

Reaction Point 1	Counselor:	What have you done in the past?
	Client:	Well, I tried my hand at several things, but then I got sick and . . .
	Counselor:	Yes, I know. Did you ever learn a trade or go to trade school?
	Client:	I started welding but . . .
	Counselor:	Right. That's out now. Is there something you're interested in now?
	Client:	I was thinking that perhaps merchandising . . .
	Counselor:	What did the vocational counselor suggest? Did he discuss your test results with you?
	Client:	He thought merchandising might be all right, but he said I'd need more education than I've had.
	Counselor:	How much have you had?
	Client:	Eight years.
	Counselor:	How old are you now?
	Client:	Going on twenty.
	Counselor:	Are both of your parents alive? Will you be staying with them when you leave us?
Reaction Point 2	Client:	I sure hope so because . . . at first . . . I'll need help . . . and . . .
	Counselor:	Do you think you'd like to go back to school for a while?
	Client:	I suppose so, but I don't know whether financially . . .
	Counselor:	Just what is your financial situation at the moment?
Reaction Point 3	Client:	Well, it isn't very good.
	Counselor:	What appeals to you about merchandising?
	Client:	Contact with people and goods, I suppose.
	Counselor:	Did you have anything else in mind?
	Client:	I like the law.
	Counselor:	Were you thinking of becoming a lawyer?

Client:	I don't know. I think Dad would like me to help him around the farm if I could . . . I mean, if the doctors agree.
Counselor:	What kind of farm does your dad have?
Client:	Practically everything but no cows.
Counselor:	Anything else besides merchandising and the law interest you?
Client:	Well, I used to do some photography.
Counselor:	That sounds interesting. What did you do?

*Reaction
Point 4*

2. Select a partner to work in your small group. Do each of the following exercises, allowing some time to share and discuss what you have experienced in the exercise with others in your group (Stevens, 1971).

(a) *Questions.* Talk with your partner for approximately two minutes using only questions. Do not attempt to answer the questions asked by your partner; only take turns asking each other questions. Every sentence must be a question. Talk with your group about how it feels to ask and be asked questions.

(b) *Questions-Variation.* Talk with your partner for approximately two minutes as question-asker. Use questions to elicit information about your partner. Your partner is, in this exercise, permitted to answer the questions briefly or may say, "pass," if s/he does not wish to answer a particular question. Switch roles after two minutes. Discuss with your group the kinds of communication which occurred and how it felt to be asked as well as to be question-asker. If positive exchanges or negative exchanges occurred between partners, discuss the possible reasons for the outcome.

(c) *Why-Because.* Initiate a conversation with your partner using the word "why" to start your question. Your partner may answer your question using the word "because" to start his/her statement. It then becomes his/her turn to ask the "why" and your turn to answer the "because." Talk with your group about this exercise. Did it make you and your partner feel "closer?"

(d) *I Know.* Talk with your partner using statements which you know to be true of him/her. ("I know you have brown eyes.") Your partner then repeats your statement and replies with something s/he knows to be true of you. Be sure your *I know* statements begin with the phrase "I know . . ."

(e) *I Assume.* Talk with your partner using statements which you assume to be true of him/her. Your partner then repeats the statement (without commenting on its validity) and also makes an "I assume that . . ." statement. Contrast this exercise with the "I know." Were there differences? How did your partner react to the two types of statements? How accurate do you think you were in the two situations? How accurate was your partner? Are assumptions helpful?

3. Tape an interview with a member of your small group, with you in the role of counselor. Ask your client about a problem or difficulty s/he had in the area of "dating."* Talk for five to seven minutes, focusing on the content of what is being said and on your listening skills. Be careful not to ask questions. Repeat the exercise with you in the role of client for another member of your small group.

---

*Many of my students have problems with this word. It is a dead give away of the era in which I grew up. Please translate this word to mean any aspect during your adolescent years about the social experimentation between males and females. Do you see how awkward *that* phrase is?

SUGGESTED ADDITIONAL READINGS

Benjamin, Alfred. *The helping interviewers*. Boston: Houghton-Mifflin, 1969.

One chapter of Benjamin's book is a strong statement about the use and misuse of questions and forms much of the foundation for the discussion in this chapter.

Dustin, Richard and George, Rickey. *Action counseling for behavior change*. New York: Intext Educational Publishers, 1973.

The behavioral stance of this particular book clearly discusses the role of the counselor as a reinforcing agent to the client. Specific behaviors of the counselor are described in terms of their reinforcing influencers.

Farwell, Gail F. et al., editors. *The counselor's handbook*. New York: Intext Educational Publishers, 1974.

In this article, Farwell clarifies the importance of the counselor in upgrading his skills and abilities once he is in practice. This whole book is an excellent source book, particularly for school counselors, on issues and practices in the professional setting.

Greenspoon, J. The reinforcing effect of two spoken sounds on the frequency of two responses, in *American Journal of Psychology*, 1955, *68*, 409-416.

This classic study by Greenspoon first pointed out the differential effects of counselor verbalizations as reinforcers and perhaps led to a blurring of the lines between theoretical approaches. Often duplicated, this study is worth reading from a historical perspective as well.

Haley, Jay. *Strategies of psychotherapy*. New York: Grune & Stratton, 1967.

Note particularly the chapter that clarifies the difference in function between therapist emphasis on *what* and emphasis on *why*.

Ivey, Allen E. *Microcounseling: Innovations in interview training*. Springfield: Charles C. Thomas, 1971.

One chapter in this book focuses on the rationale for training in specific skills.

London, P. *The modes and morals of psychotherapy*. New York: Holt, Rinehart and Winston, 1964.

This is a classic and imminently readable book which discusses the differences and similarities between various schools of psychotherapy and the ethical issues involved in each as well as the ethical issues generated by chauvinism.

Klas, L. and Peters, Herman, J. Counseling interviewer techniques: A comparison of theory and practice, in *Counselor Education and Supervision*, 1973, *13*, 137-143.

This is a summary and description of over sixty techniques and a discussion of overlap across theoretical approaches.

Matarazzo, Ruth G. Research on the teaching and learning of psychotherapeutic skills, in Garfield, S. and Bergin, A., editors, *Handbook of psychotherapy and behavior change*. New York: John Wiley and Sons, in press.

This is an excellent summary of research into the effectiveness of the skill-building approach, with particular emphasis on Ivey's microcounseling approach and the Carkhuff facilitative conditions. Matarazzo critiques the format of many of the research methodologies and points out the lack of equivalent research into the effectiveness of more advanced psychotherapeutic skills.

Paul, I. H. *Letters to Simon*. New York: International University Press, 1973.

This is nice reading, written in the form of an experienced therapist writing informally to a novice on many issues — including silence and technique.

Prazak, Gary. Accountability for counseling programs, in Krumboltz, John, D. and Thoresen, Carl E., editors, *Counseling methods*. New York: Holt, Rinehart and Winston, 1976.

This is a good discussion of accountability and what it translates to in the professional setting. Some practical applications of the concept are suggested.

Ruesch, Jurgen. *Therapeutic communication*. New York: W. W. Norton, 1961.

An early successful attempt to integrate psychotherapy with communications theory, Ruesch introduces the concept of "immediacy" — that of matching counselor response to the tone of the client statement. His book is filled with excellent examples of his style and approach to counseling.

Stevens, John O. *Awareness: Exploring, experimenting and experiencing*. Moab, Utah: Real People Press, 1971.

Many of the experiences in this text are borrowed or adapted from Stevens' humanistically-oriented book. All of the exercises are fascinating; many can be used for personal enrichment as well as interpersonal understanding. Chapter Three has the most directly relevant exercises; its title is "Communication with Others."

Truax, C. B. and Mitchell, Kevin M. Research on certain therapist interpersonal skills in relation to process and outcome, in Bergin, Allen E. and Garfield, Sol L., editors, *Handbook of psychotherapy and behavior change* (first edition). New York: John Wiley and Sons, 1971.

This is an excellent summary of the relational process skills research conducted, primarily, by Truax and Carkhuff and their associates. This article is particularly interesting for its summary of the investigation by Truax into the reinforcing behaviors of Carl Rogers with a long-term client.

4

The Understanding of Content

The RELATIONSHIP of CONTENT to LISTENING

Although the focus in our approach to therapeutic communication in counseling is on the *process* of communication and the interaction between counselor and client, there are unique characteristics that each participant brings to the session. The counselor, at this point in our training sequence, should be bringing some listening skills to the interview. The client brings his/her problems. The question then arises: What does the counselor listen to? A simple answer is that the counselor listens to *everything* — expressed and unexpressed, verbal and nonverbal, external and internal.

This too can be approached sequentially and in fractions of the whole. The sequential approach, interestingly, closely parallels the sequence of relational development with each client. At beginning stages of the relationship — in earlier sessions — the counselor should be focusing on getting the *client's* story, the client's view of his/her inner and outer world. The first step in training oneself to hear everything is an internal step: The counselor must give him/herself permission to hear the content of the *client's* story.

Kell and Mueller (1966) speak of compacted experiences in clients. The client has compacted and compressed his/her experiences, usually but not always at the cost of the emotional response to those experiences. It is the counselor's function in early stages of the relationship to help the client expand those experiences to the point where both participants in the interaction feel fairly certain that understanding has been achieved. The counselor needs to recognize that counselor messages to the client serve as a feedback system to the client. In representing his/her problems to the counselor, the client is adept at "scanning" the counselor, that is, watching the counselor for cues as to how s/he is coming across, how s/he is being received.

This is not unique to the counseling relationship. The client

brings all previous interpersonal experiences to the counseling relationship. The client has developed a style of interaction which generally elicits a certain kind of response, one we will call "social"
(Beier, 1966), from the people in his/her environment. This style,
and its related style of interpersonal reactions, may be totally ineffective and unsatisfying, yet the client continues to attempt the same
behaviors, rather than change the style. The client's first attempt at
change is very likely the seeking of counseling.

Obviously, it is imperative that the counselor does not reinforce
the same style that the client is finding to be inadequate and unsatisfying by giving the "social" response. The counselor's role at this
stage is to provide the most neutral cues possible to the client, asocial
responses so that the client is free to describe his/her own reality
without having to modify it to fit the counselor's reactions.

A good example of this process lies in the client who comes to
counseling with a tragic story. If, while the client is relating, I as
counselor react with sympathy or shock or jump to conclusions
about how the client is feeling, I have responded in the social way.
My responses are a function of me and my emotions and are not a
function of the relationship (or my skills). Only if I open myself to
the content — both expressed and unexpressed — can I allow myself
the sensitivity to be aware of my perceptions — how the client is
relating the story, the words which are chosen to express the story,
the presence of affect, and how I *might* have felt in that situation.
I place my own emotional responses on hold, on reserve, until I
am sure that I have a clear understanding. Only then am I a participant — and a skilled one at that — who can effect change in my
client's representations.

At the content level of interaction (Level One in our paradigm),
the counselor is plainly "tuning in" — much like on a radio dial, cut-
ting back on interference which is the kind Sathre et al. (1973) discuss, and focusing attention on the client's representation of his/her
world. The client usually needs some time and some neutral assistance from the counselor to expand this compacted picture.

The INTERACTIONAL APPROACH

Viewing the counseling interaction as a feedback system rather
than as a linear influence model allows the counselor to examine
ways that s/he is affected by the client's messages. It is apparent that
the counselor does *not* maintain the same style of interaction and/or
helping behaviors across clients. Rogers et al. (1967) point out
that such qualities as empathy and non-possessive warmth vary
broadly from client to client Thus, the quality of the interaction

between the two participants would seem to be more than the separate qualities of each of the participants.

Understanding the client's message can be beneficial in that it leads to understanding the *effect* of the client's message on the counselor.

If we reduce the client's message to a stimulus and the counselor's message to a response, we at least are acknowledging the *evoking* nature of the client's remarks (Danzinger, 1976). The client makes statements in order to elicit a response from the counselor. The nature of that response is dependent on how much emotion is aroused within the counselor — emotion that has little or no bearing on the relationship and perhaps considerable bearing on (a) the social response being elicited from the client and (b) emotional re-actions in the counselor to content being expressed.

The *social response* is a broad term for the class of behaviors which the client elicits in his/her everyday life from significant re-lationships. Obviously, the social response is not particularly helpful or the client wouldn't be seeking professional assistance. Frequently the social response only serves to reinforce those representations of experiences which the client needs to change. Examples of the social response range from sympathy to changing the subject to questions probing the reasons for the client's behavior. All of these are "ex-pected" by the client and serve as reinforcers for more of the same behaviors which s/he is emitting or for maintaining the belief that his/her experiences may in fact be overwhelming and s/he had better keep them to him/herself.

The *asocial response* is purposefully neutral and permits further exploration while subtly encouraging the client to try new behaviors. The asocial response repeats the content, minimally encourages, and does not provide immediate feedback of the kind which can be uti-lized by the client to modify and censor his/her own speech. The client's representation is allowed to expand and continue.

PERSUASION of the COUNSELOR — "Getting Hooked"

Frequently words and topics are introduced by the client which arouse emotional reactions in the counselor. As such, they are words which the counselor should pay attention to and register, perhaps filing them away for later use (either within that counselor/client re-lationship or within him/herself as an area which is still serving as interference to effective listening).

The client who walks in, sits down and describes him/herself as a parolee who has been convicted and imprisoned for murdering his wife/her husband is very aware of the kind of response this information usually elicits from people. If the counselor squirms, reacts visibly or vocally to this information, s/he has become "hooked" by the content expressed, and has given the client strong cues about modifying and censoring his/her speech (or exactly what topic renders the counselor inoperable). While this is perhaps an exaggerated example, it does serve to stress the dynamics of persuasive messages, messages which cause emotional reactions in the counselor. Those reactions interfere with the counselor's ability to be helpful to the client. In this example, the counselor has already reacted and the client has yet to state his/her problem or his/her reasons for seeking counseling.

Listening, as we are defining it here, is in itself an asocial response. Giving permission, through use of neutral statements, to the client to expand the compacted experience with minimal concern about the reactions in his/her listener, is not the usual interaction between people. For a multitude of reasons, interpersonal interactions are not characterized by quality listening behaviors in the participants. Sathre et al. (1973) have pointed this out by describing differing kinds of listening, kinds of listening which we as individuals apply to the demands of differing situations. These kinds of listening include ". . . appreciative listening, conversational listening, courteous listening, and listening to indicate love or respect. Appreciative listening is listening to anything which pleases us — concerts, radio, plays, stories, poetry, television, etc." Little effort is required. Our interest is usually held because our interest has been stimulated. The sounds are pleasureable and, while they may stimulate many responses within us, a response is not required. We generally do not react in social situations with this kind of listening. By nature, it is an asocial response.

Conversational social listening has been discussed in a previous chapter. The interest level will vary sometimes with the topic and sometimes depending on the closeness of the relationship between the speaker and the listener. For example, listening to a fellow traveler on a bus generally does not involve the same interest level as listening to our close friends, yet both do not *require* a commitment on the part of the listener. If the subject matter is interesting, the listener finds it relatively simple to stay tuned in; if not, the listener responds much as s/he would to a situation involving appreciative listening — s/he changes the subject (channel) or leaves the area.

Courteous listening is "somewhat similar, except that we do less talking and more listening, as when we listen to a guest expound on his/her views, even though we may not really be interested (Sathre et al, 1973)." The parallel here to social listening is remarkable. While we may give all of the outward indications of listening, frequently, because our interest is low, we have changed the subjects in our heads and are in reality thinking of something else. The eyes may become glazed, the mind drifts off, the channel is no longer open.

Listening to communicate love or respect demands a little more energy from the listener. The implication here is that the speaker and the listener have a closer relationship, and although the subject matter may not be important to the listener, the speaker is. The listener then makes an attempt to understand the meaning *to the speaker* of the subject being discussed. The listener may not be personally interested in foreign cars, the stock market, the science project at school, the new recipe for banana nut bread, but s/he is interested in the speaker and therefore in what significance that topic holds for the speaker. The listener listening in a counseling relationship is of course most similar to the situations of appreciation (without changing the channel) and of listening to communicate love and respect. The subject matter is even more critical, because it usually involves life experiences that are of great importance to the speaker. Adequate understanding of the significance of those life experiences to the speaker is basic to understanding the unique life space of the client.

This quality of listening or the attitude of listening conveyed to the client is an asocial response; it implies that the listener will make every effort to not turn that channel, to stay focused on the messages s/he is receiving, and to not interrupt the speaker's flow with irrelevancies, contradictory opinions or diversions into new topic areas.

The verbal responses the counselor makes are asocial responses in that they do not replicate conversational responses the client may be receiving in his/her environment. They do not reinforce a style of interaction in the client which may no longer be satisfying or healthy. They do not give feedback cues to the client which can be used to modify or censor the client's speech.

SOME THINGS the COUNSELOR CAN LISTEN TO

A.   Determining Situational Stress

In discussing the responses the client has learned to elicit from others within his/her environment, we have alluded to the view of the client as a person within a social system, rather than an isolated individual with isolated problems. It seems to be appropriate to view the client in this manner and when listening to the client, to pay particular attention to information about the social system around the client. What significant others are in the client's life? How do they seem to reinforce or exacerbate the client's behaviors? What kinds of behaviors and attitudes does the client seem to expect from these people within his/her system?

These are overview kinds of questions and should not, of course, be asked directly. They may not be answered within the first hour or within several hours of initial contact, yet they are informational areas which the counselor should be alert to, filing them away to be added to the counselor's sense of understanding the client's world. The significant others in the client's life may well be adding to the client's situational stress. As well, the client's style of interaction with his/her environment may be eliciting the exact kind of responses from those significant others which add to the situational stress.

B.   Attempted Solutions

Frequently, in an environment such as the counseling interview, where the client is free to expand his/her compacted experiences, s/he will describe attempts at solving his/her problems and how the client has attempted to handle unsolved problems in the past. This, too, is information the counselor should be alert to in developing understanding of the client's style. Patterns of behavior which can be best described as "more of the same" have been detailed by Watzlawick, Weakland and Fisch (1974). These types of behavior patterns are additional cues which the counselor should register and use to develop and expand understanding of the client.

C.   Conflicting Messages

The counselor, at early stages of the interview, should also be alert to those messages which come from the client — which conflict in some real or apparent manner. Conflicting messages may simply occur as part of the internal logic of the client's representation. Described reactions to events may seem (to the alert counselor) inappropriate or unexpected. Affect which is described may be described with contradictory accompanying affect. Changes in topic may be abrupt and startling. These types of content messages, while parhaps *not* part of the "plot", are certainly cues for the counselor to use as potential sources of understanding.

In the same manner that the counselor should be alert to conflicting messages in the style of representation, s/he should also be alert to areas within the client's life — within the representation itself — that are conflicted *and* how those conflicts make the counselor feel. In other words, what responses are elicited by the client or the counselor when the client describes the conflicted areas of his/her life? Double-binds, for example, (Bateson et al., 1956) are areas of conflict which when described sometimes elicit feelings of powerlessness and defeat in the counselor. Those are reactions which are helpful to the counselor's developing understanding.

Those are reactions which are helpful to the counselor's developing understanding.

CONTENT RESPONSES

The attentiveness of the counselor to factors of situational stress, attempted solutions and conflicting messages are examples of directions the counselor's listening behavior can take. Content responses, responses which are neutral and asocial in nature assist the client in representing his/her world with minimal restriction or modification. Accurately communicating understanding of the client's message through use content responses serves the purpose of fostering growth of the relationship without communicating personal reactions or value judgments to the client.

Content responses which communicate understanding while at the same time allow the counselor to check his/her perceptions and understanding of the client's representation are paraphrasing and summarization.

A.   Paraphrasing

Paraphrasing is basically a form of the restatement, except the words used are not the exact words utilized by the client. The meaning of the response should be close, if not interchangeable, with the meaning of the client's statement. The problems of "decoding" are introduced at this point, with the weight of the responsibility on the counselor to *accurately understand* what is being communicated. Accurate paraphrasing communicates this understanding to the client and does much to increase the quality of the counseling relationship. Paraphrasing is basically a continuing response, used to continue the client's verbalizations and explorations, as well as indicating close listening by the counselor.

Examples: (a)   Client: I lost my job and don't know what to do.

Counselor: You're out of work.

Purpose: Summarizes the client's experience.

(b)   Client: I can't decide what to do about the baby.

Counselor: It's like you can't make up your mind.

Purpose: Paraphrases the indecision of the client.

B.   Summarization

Summarization is an extended form of the restatement. In it two or more thoughts are restated or paraphrased, rather than just one. In this way the selectivity of the restatement is sometimes avoided. The restatement summarization is also especially effective at the end of the counseling session.

Example: Client: . . . and that's about it.

                 Counselor: Let's see if I understand what you've been saying. You're unhappy with your job and don't think it's a good idea to leave it just now with your wife in the hospital. In addition, your mother is trying to talk you into moving in with her. Is that it?

                 Purpose: Organizes the content of the client's words.

C.   Reintroducing Old Material

Occasionally a previously introduced topic will become significant by its very absence from later sessions. The client may studiously avoid the area of high inner conflict because it is either so anxiety-provoking or it was handled poorly in an earlier session. I am reminded of an occasion where a female student discussed her roommate problem early in a counseling relationship, received some practical advice and then did not bring up the topic again. Instead she verbalized a lot about many different topics, not to any depth, for four consecutive sessions. At the fifth session, during a pause by the client to catch her breath, the counselor leaned forward and stated, "I haven't heard much about the roommate lately." The client promptly burst into tears and related the very real pressure she was feeling in the relationship with her roommate. The advice hadn't worked.

Ordinarily, it is the client's responsibility to discuss the topics of concern to him/her; occasionally the counselor, by his/her actions, has limited those topics and must operate to correct the flow of content. The counselor also needs to listen to his/her own sense of timing.

D.   Ignoring

Occasionally there occur moments when the wisest recourse open to the counselor is deliberate ignoring of content. Situations when this occurs seem to be associated with little relevance to what *seems* to be the topic under consideration or an attempt on the part of the counselor not to reinforce certain aspects of the described behavior. As well, the material might be of the "red flag" variety, intended by the client to keep the counselor away from more relevant issues. The material selected to be ignored should, of course, be stored as input and perhaps utilized at a later time when its meaning to the client and the counselor is a little more distinct. The rationale for using this counselor response should be fairly clear in the counselor's mind.

ACTIVITIES

1. Using the video equipment, if possible, tape an interview with a member of your small group, with you in the role of counselor. Ask your client about a problem or difficulty s/he had in his/her relationship with his/her parents. Ask the other members of your small group to observe the taping session and give you feedback on your verbal and nonverbal communication of accurate understanding. Talk for about five to seven minutes, focusing on the content of what is being said and on listening skills, use of silence, restatements and paraphrases. Be careful not to ask questions. Repeat the exercise with you in the role of client for another member of your small group. Write down the session as you remember it. What information did you store? How did you feel during the interview?

2. Replay your tape and listen to the responses you made. How confident do you sound? What kind of responses do you tend to use? Count and list the different responses you made. An example follows. Turn this simplified tape analysis in at the same time you play your tape for the instructor.

			Response Type
Example:	Counselor:	Could you tell me something about your parents?	General Lead
	Counselor:	Umm-hmmm.	Minimal Encouragement
	Counselor:	You lived in Chicago.	Restatement
	Counselor:	Catholics have the same restrictions.	Informing
	Counselor:	What did you do then?	Question

After this tape analysis is complete, compare it with your notes taken after the interview.

SUGGESTED ADDITIONAL READINGS

Andrews, John. Personal change and intervention style, in *Journal of Humanistic Psychology*, 1977, *17*, 3, 41-63.

Andrews clarifies the relationship between the social response (which he calls "negative feedback") and the maintenance of faulty and maladaptive self-definitions. This is then formulated into a series of growth-promoting interventions which utilize the individual's "maintenance energies" for new behaviors and personal change. This interesting approach is applied to a film of three major therapists.

Bateson, G., Jackson, D. D., Haley, J. and Weakland, J. Toward a theory of schizophrenia, in *Behavioral Science*, 1956, *1*, 251-264.

For the clearest explanation of the double-bind hypothesis, the original source by Bateson and his colleagues still exceeds the quality set for theoretical exposition. It is fascinating reading.

Beier, Ernst G. *The silent language of psychotherapy*. Chicago: Aldine Publishing Co., 1966.

The communications theory approach to psychotherapy is well represented by this book. Beier maintains he is combining behavioral techniques with a psychoanalytic approach, but his work on the asocial message is invaluable for understanding communication between therapist and client.

Danzinger, Kurt. *Interpersonal communication*. New York: Pergamon Press, Inc., 1976.

Danzinger also considers the social and asocial message in this clearly written introductory text to communications theory. The reciprocal impact of client messages on the counselor is explored in Chapter Six. Chapter Four is a fine source on nonverbal communication.

Kell, Bill L. and Mueller, William J. *Impact and change: A study of counseling relationships*. New York: Appleton-Century-Crofts, 1966.

Although written primarily for supervisiors of counselors-in-training, this excellent and difficult book is a good source for gaining an understanding of the reciprocal influence in the counseling relationship.

Rogers, C. R., Gendlin, G. I., Kresler, D. V. and Truax, C. B. *The therapeutic relationship and its impact: A study of psychotherapy with schizophrenia*. Madison: University of Wisconsin Press, 1967.

Particularly noteworthy is the description of the variation in qualities like warmth, empathy and genuineness with therapists across different clients, lending considerable support to the reciprocal influence model.

Ruesch, J. and Bateson, G. *Communication: The social matrix of psychiatry*. New York: W. W. Norton, 1951.

For a basic approach to the communications model of counseling, therapy and psychiatry, this book is highly useful.

Sathre, Freda S., Olson, Ray W. and Whitney, Clarissa I. *Let's talk*. Glenview: Scott, Foresman & Co., 1973.

This is an introductory text on the process of interpersonal communication and is written in a lively style. It provides a nice foundation for some of the more difficult books recommended to the beginning counselor.

Watzlawick, P., Weakland, John and Fisch, Dick. *Change: Principles of problem formation and problem resolution*, N. Y.: W. W. Norton & Co., 1974.

See Sathre first. This book is complex in its treatment of the communications model, but the mathematical principles included in Chapter One can be skipped with no loss to understanding. It is an interesting perspective on changing behavior.

PART II: Level Two Interactions

5

The Hidden Realm of Feeling

SUBJECTIVE EXPERIENCE

If there is one developmental task children in Western culture master it is the rather difficult one of learning to hide their feelings. From toddler age to adolescence, children are admonished to not feel the way they are feeling — told not to cry, to be grown-up and brave, told not to express their anger or disappointment. Frequently, they are told how they should be feeling, again with the implication that the feelings they are experiencing are inappropriate or wrong. Our children learn from parents, teachers and other children to keep their feelings to themselves. Some of them master an additional skill and keep their feelings from themselves as well.

Historically, Americans have precedent for this educational emphasis on keeping feelings under wraps. Historically, Americans have been an instrumental society, priding themselves on what was useful. Technological advances came faster than people could process them. Advances were evaluated on their usefulness. This utilitarian emphasis extended to the presentation of self as a commodity. The "Man in the Gray Flannel Suit" spread from Madison Avenue in New York to the West Coast because he was aggressive, quick to make decisions, other-directed and useful. A utilitarian emphasis on things, thoughts, and thinking through solutions largely neglected the subjective, more personal side of experiencing. Feelings were simply not very important. Feelings were not useful. And feelings tended to interfere with business.

Fortunately, or unfortunately for many of us, our feelings just didn't disappear after we learned to hide them. They hung around, affecting us at inappropriate moments, causing angry flare-ups over trivial things, disproportionate sadness over minor disappointments, tension and anxiety at moments when we most wished to maintain our control. They tended to leak through in spite of our best efforts. Yet still we tried to hide them, ignored them and pretended they did not exist. How could anything we were supposed to hide have any value?

The value of the subjective side of experience was noticed by several authors and psychologists who became concerned about the alienation from self which resulted from the one-sided personality. Humanistic psychology noisily shouted warnings to the public about surface-level communication, loss of identity, the meaning of existence, man/woman's search for meaning. The pressure was on, and selected groups responded, almost gratefully, to a view of man/woman as a whole person.

Yet, as Americans, we responded in many ways as to a fad, a new bandwagon to ride. We brought with us our needs to objectify and to make the bandwagon useful. Feelings became something to identify, label and sort (sometimes even exchanged on the open market), as if in finding names for our feelings we had found solutions to all our troubles. The trend grew towards trying to make life an unending series of sensations and feelings, now ignoring the cognitive aspect of ourselves and failing to process this new-found tool to understanding. My sense is that for some the realm of feelings is just another commodity.

Many retreated from this game of objectifying and found the content mode, the "thinking-man's mode", much easier to adjust to. Many others continue to dabble with their new toy, seeking more and more novel experiences and sensations in their lives. Either mode of operation is inadequate of itself. Communication on a surface level continues to leave great gaps in experiencing and satisfaction. Recognition that this is the incomplete life is fairly easy, yet the alternative may be frightening because it is viewed as an either/or choice. Oddly, those who advocate the feeling realm as a primary state do not recognize their one-sidedness, their own separation from self. As Buber points out, "That feelings yield no personal life is understood only by a few, for the most personal life of all (appears to) reside in feelings, and if, like the modern man you have learned to concern yourself wholly with your own feelings, despair at their unreality will not readily instruct you in a better way — for despair itself is also an interesting feeling."

The RELATIONSHIP of FEELING and CONTENT

Viewing feelings on one end of a continuum in opposition to content (thinking) on the other may be very artificial. This either/or duality may have been imposed by cultural and historical pressures toward emphasis of one mode over and at the expense of the other.

An alternative view can be suggested. It may be that all experiences are layered events, the cognitive being our objective understanding is aided and modified by our personal language system — what is stored by us to be communicated to others. Beneath that layer (which hypothetically could vary in thickness) is a second layer, that of our inner reactions and the feeling states which are associated with the event.

The first layer is generally rich with words. It is easy to select the wanted words from a field of so many to describe the event in a content way. If our training as children in hiding our feelings has been very successful it is a thick layer (probably of more words), and our ability to find the feelings associated with the event is hindered. If our learning experiences in exploring those feelings have been painful or limited to objectifying the associated feelings, the layer may be calloused and toughened in many places. Asking some people how they feel in these circumstances may be akin to asking them to speak a foreign language. We must utilize other channels of communication to understand the feeling layer of the message.

People go to great pains to demonstrate the skills they have mastered in concealing their feelings. Verbally they address to social morés and do not violate the cultural taboos on verbally expressing feelings, yet still these feelings are expressed. Through the "leaking" of nonverbal cues, communication extends beyond verbal expression, and the listener "picks up" messages about how the speaker feels about his/her message. The accuracy of sensing how the speaker feels is, of course, variable within a range of boundaries imposed by the simple fact that we all learn to communicate feelings in the same way. Recent studies by Mehrabian (1967, 1969, 1970a and 1970b) and others indicate that whether or not accuracy or validity is a factor, people tend to pay *more* attention to nonverbal cues than to verbal ones. Mehrabian and his researchers found that the impact of the facial expression is greater than the impact of the tone of voice and, to a much lesser degree, finally the words themselves. The message will be interpreted on the basis not of what has been said (representation) but how it has been said (presentation). This is intriguing in its own way, but especially since we receive no formalized instruction in the use of these nonverbal cues. Most of them are received and sent at a level below our awareness.

Wiener and Mehrabian (1968) believe this reliance on other channels is basic to the process of communication between people. "It is assumed that the human organism cannot totally "conceal" emotion — that emotion denied expression in one channel finds another outlet. . . . Feelings are conveyed less overtly (and often without conscious volition) by nonverbal behaviors. . . They assume a greater significance to many who rely more on these less-censored expressions. The de-emphasis of nonverbal communication in education helps to perpetuate a situation in which socially unacceptable feelings must be expressed in behaviors other than speech and cannot be recognized "officially" as part of a person's communication. We learn to express a variety of feelings in these more subtle ways and avoid detractable transgression of the social norms."

In other words, feelings *are* expressed in culturally-learned, informally-learned ways of communicating — the nonverbal channels. It is these access routes to the emotional reactions and inner feeling states that counselors must be particularly aware of.

Awareness, of course, is a double-edged sword. Not only is it an obvious access route to understanding the client, but it is a source of "leaking" that must be neutralized in the counselor. That is, the counselor has been subjected to the same social learning process and "leaks" nonverbal cues which indicate emotional reactions of the counselor to the client's message. These cues serve as reinforcers of the client's existing patterns.

At the second level of communication it is hypothesized that feelings associated with the content are expressed primarily through nonverbal channels.

UNDERSTANDING the CLIENT'S FEELINGS

A.   Recognizing the Unverbalized.

Content skills are invaluable in recognizing the client's verbalized feelings. When a client uses words to describe feeling states, these words should be picked up, restated with matching inflection (or at least *not* exaggerated inflection) or paraphrased using words of interchangeable value. Much of the time at this level of communication, however, the counselor must rely on nonverbal channels of expression.

There have been numerous aspects of communication which have been researched and found to be valid sources of information about (a) the nature of the relationship between speaker and listener and (b) the feelings the speaker has about the message expressed. Danzinger (1976) summarizes these communication channels and the major research. The following is a brief summary of Danzinger's sources of information. The interested reader is referred to the sources at the end of this chapter for a fuller exposition of channels and supporting research.

1.   *Proxemics* is defined as the study of physical distance between persons. The distance decreases with the closeness of the relationship and increases when the feelings of the participants become negative. This theorem is limited to the range of personal distance (18 inches to 3 feet) which has been found to be most comfortable

for Americans. It is also modified by location. (It is easier to be comfortable with close proximity if the room is small; conversely, in a large auditorium where acoustics are poor, the participants in a conversation may move closer to one another to be heard.)

2. *Posture* refers to the degree of leaning toward one another in a conversational dyad. If the feelings are positive, there is a tendency to lean toward the other. If the feelings are negative, the posture stiffens and/or leans away. A related aspect of posture is found between two people who perceive each other as being of unequal status. The person with the most perceived power (status) will be the most physically relaxed.

3. *Paralanguage* refers to a large class of vocal behaviors which are not strictly part of the verbalized language. These vocal behaviors include pitch (which rises with the rise in negative feelings), and volume (which rises with some negative feelings, like anger, and lowers with others, like distress, sorrow, shame). Rate of speech varies with the amount of negative feelings. Generally, it slows down and becomes halting, the higher the negative feeling associated with the content or the relationship. Hesitations and tripping over words have been found to be associated with levels of anxiety. Laughter, giggles, sighs, incomplete phrases separated by pauses — all of these communicate feelings about the message being conveyed.

4. *Gaze direction* (eye contact) tends to increase with the positive feelings in a relationship or with positive feelings generated about the topic. It decreases with negative feelings. Some topics generate such discomfort that eye contact is completely suspended. Eye contact is also used as an avenue of reassurance. This channel of communication may be the one most modified by cultural differences. Certain minority groups, for example, believe it is rude to directly meet the gaze of anyone other than one's intimate.

5. *Movements.* The area of bodily movement may well be the most widely talked about in the psychology of these channels of communication. All kinds of feeling states have been attributed to whether or not an individual crosses his/her arms (or legs or wrists). Rather than any one specific bodily movement, the counselor should be aware of shifts in movement, using the hands to punctuate, emphasize, underscore the meaning of the message.

6. *Facial expressions.* Since the facial expression is the number one source of information about inner feeling states, it goes without saying that the counselor should be alert to the facial expression accompanying the message. Does it coincide with the message or is it conveying another unrelated or contradictory feeling?

These sensory channels of information work together to give us an interrelated picture of how the content — the verbal representation of events — is presented *affectively*. Not only should the counselor be aware of how the client is emotionally presenting his/her experiences but the counselor should also be filing away information as to how the counselor is affected by these other sensory input.

B.   Empathy

The ability to recognize and understand the inner feelings of another is the counselor attribute known as empathy. Empathy is not a quality that comes out of the air. Obviously, many of the nonverbal signals we have described serve as vehicles for accurate transmission of inner feelings to another person. Being alert to those signals is one way of recognizing feelings. Most of us have some skill in recognition simply because we live in a culture where the communication of feelings is not advocated at a verbal level, and therefore most of us have had to rely on our abilities to pick up feelings on the basis of these cues. Those who recognize these cues most readily are said to be high in empathy.

Interestingly, most of the time we use these cues without being conscious of them. Because we've all been exposed to the same culture we learned to recognize these cues as a way of attempting to understand the feelings of others — feelings which usually are not verbally expressed. Our skill in picking up these cues can be improved with training and practice. Therefore, each of us can increase our ability to be empathic.

Empathy is often confused with sympathy. The two emotions arise from very different sources and are processed differently inside the individual. As we have stated, empathy is dependent on the receiver's ability to pick up cues which are sent by another person. Sympathy arises from the receiver picking up cues which occur *internally,* as a result of content being expressed. The empathic listener tries to move closer to the sender, either in actuality by physically approaching or figuratively, by attempting to receive even more cues and messages, i.e., increasing understanding. The sympathetic listener is dealing with his/her own messages internally and usually will distance further from the sender, either by moving away or by focusing even more specifically on content. This will trigger more internal responses which probably will have very little to do with the emotions of the sender.

Most of us react in a sympathetic way to situations and events which feel too overwhelming to us. The crippled beggar on the corner, the victim in the news story of a tornado — each of these events are probably outside of our experiences, and we distance ourselves as quickly as possible.

C.   Empathy in Counseling

In counseling situations we may hear stories which feel exceedingly painful to us. (Notice that the pain is ours and may have very little to do with the feelings our client may be experiencing.) We might "file" that reaction too, and then go back to the business of listening to our client to find out through attending to the client's story *and* his/her nonverbal signals how *s/he* feels.

Part of the task of developing empathy is increasing our ability to recognize the cues which are sent.   There is an additional component.   Understanding those cues and communicating that understanding to our client requires the addition of new skills to our repertoire.

These additional skills foster the growth of the counseling relationship in significant increments.   As the client grows in belief that the counselor is not overwhelmed, or reassuring, or distancing him/her but is accurately receiving the client's messages, both expressed and unexpressed, the client finds it easier to explore in depth. S/He also finds it a novel experience — one that fosters the development of new responses in him/her — because the social response is to reassure, or to be overwhelmed by negative arousal. How *truly* reassuring it must be to relate a story, to represent a painful experience, one that has seemed overwhelming in its affect to us and to find our listener accepts it and understands it.   There is an implied non-judgmental stance in this kind of listening because the process of judging is an internal one, based on the listener's range of experiences and values, and our hypothetical counselor-listener perhaps is too busy trying to improve the accuracy of his/her understanding to take the time to internally judge another's experience.

EXPLORATORY RESPONSES — Introducing Feeling

The timing of the Level Two response is critical. If introduced too rapidly in a relationship, the counselor is probably operating on limited data (from fewer sources in content and affective nonverbal realms) and takes a high risk of being off-base.   The counselor may also find s/he is bringing to awareness feelings that the client is unable or unwilling to express in what seems to the client to be another "social" setting.   The best cue to the correctness of the counselor's timing that the counselor has is when the client is expressing some feelings verbally as well.   The counselor then can follow the client's lead and include those feelings in the exchange.   As well, s/he can introduce a few that have not been expressed.   Other clients may be very hesitant to express feelings in any form.   The counselor has some specialized skills that are helpful to this kind of client.   They will be introduced in the next chapter.

SKILLS at Level Two

A. *Utilizing Content Responses.* The counselor basically re-states the expressed experience of the client, both to acknowledge recognition of that experience and to assist the client in continuing. These responses are identical to restatements except that their focus is on the feeling words utilized by the client. The tone of the words used should match the tone used by the client.

Example: Client: I have a hard time with tests. I don't seem to do well. I just get so nervous before a test and then I go in and blow it.

Counselor: You feel nervous before a test.

Purpose: To pick up and reinforce the feeling component of the message.

B. *Reflection of feeling* is continuing response, inviting fur-ther exploration on the part of the client. This technique helps to bring problems and their associated feelings into focus without the client feeling pushed or probed. Inaccurate reflections of feeling serve to distance the counseling relationship because the client feels less understood; s/he feels that the counselor has "missed" the essence of his/her communication. Inaccurate reflections are usually caused by a too-previous leap into the realm of feelings without adequate "building" on content understanding. Accurate reflections occur when the counselor in fact has an adequate picture of the client's inner world.

Example: Client: I wish I could ask about my grade in the course, but the teacher seems so busy.

Counselor: Sounds like you feel the teacher has no time for you.

Purpose: To communicate understanding of the client's feelings.

C. *Interchangeable Responses.* As the counselor grows in experience, s/he can recognize the feeling expressed and rather than using that exact response, shift to another word for the same feeling. Frequently, the direction of the shift will improve the accuracy of the identified feeling, that is, in the process of discarding our first response we shift to one which is closer to the client's actual exper-iencing, simply because we may be picking up more nonverbal mes-sages than we are consciously aware of. Our rejection of the con-scious, "easy" response forces us to utilize our own processing of the client's message. The words appear interchangeable, and yet the subtle differences between them are usually in the client's favor.

Example: Client: I just don't feel good about anything;
there's nothing that involves me and I'm
tired of being bored.

Counselor: (1) You feel outside of life.
(2) You feel excluded by life.

Purpose: To reflect accurately the feeling being expressed.
(The second choice response may, in fact, be
closer to the client's experience.)

ACTIVITIES

1. *Nonverbal Cancelling* (Stevens, 1971). Choose a partner in
your small group and sit down facing each other. Discuss a topic of
current interest to you (your classes, politics, religion, finances) and
deliberately cancel the meaning of everything you say with gestures,
facial expression, tone of voice or any other nonverbal behavior. Be
aware of how you feel as you do this. Switch roles, listening to your
partner discuss something of interest to him/her. Be aware of how
you feel as you listen. Discuss the experience with your partner.
How did you cancel your message? What nonverbal channels did you
use? Are you aware of having paired the nonverbal cancelling messages with your messages in the past? What did you notice about
your partner's behavior?

2. *Diary of Feelings.* Keep a brief record of your feelings
during a twenty-four hour period. Try to record each feeling as soon
after it occurs as possible *or* "check" yourself every two hours for a
reading on your feeling state and record your observations. As you
list the feeling you are aware of, describe its nonverbal partners and
also record the behaviors which would be observed by others. Then
take a moment to determine if a secondary feeling is there. If so, record it. A sample chart follows:

Time	Feeling	Observable Behavior	Nonverbal Partners	Secondary Feeling
2:00 P.M.	Tired	Walking slowly, eyes burning, shoulders aching	Body slumped, head bent over, mouth tense	Irritation

3. Using video equipment (if possible) tape an interview with
a member of your small group, with you in the role of counselor.
Ask your client about a problem or difficulty s/he has had in a relationship with his/her siblings (or lack of siblings). Ask the members
of your small group to observe the taping session and give you and
your partner feedback on your nonverbal communication. Talk for
about five to seven minutes, focusing on the client's expression of
any feelings and utilizing the new skills at this level when appropriate.

SUGGESTED ADDITIONAL READINGS

Beier, Ernst and Valens, Evans. *People-reading*. New York: Stein and Day, 1975.

Designed for popular sales markets, this book offers an updated and well-researched approach to the usefulness of nonverbal channels and the persuasive messages we are all bombarded with.

Buber, Martin. *I and thou*. New York: Charles Scribner's Sons, 1958.

Buber's philosophy and approach to relating to others and to relatedness in general is beautifully written and a model for respecting and valuing others. He also indicates the necessity for balance in relationships between I-it (objective) and I-thou (subjective), and clarifies that life cannot be lived fully at either extreme without experiencing both modes.

Bugental, Daphne E., Kaswan, Jaques W. and Love, Leonore R. Perception of contradictory meanings conveyed by verbal and nonverbal channels, in *Journal of Personality and Social Psychology*, 1970, *16*, 4, 647-655.

Bugental and associates describe an experiment using "joking" or sarcasm paired with contradictory nonverbal messages. They found support for the contention that conflicted messages are rated more negatively and that nonverbal cues may be the stronger determinant of the interpretation by the listener.

Cochrane, Carolyn I. Development of a measure of empathic communication, in *Psychotherapy*, 1974, *11*, 1, 41-47.

In the process of attempting to measure the elusive concept of empathy, Cochrane does an interesting job of defining some of its components and clarifying the concept itself.

Danzinger, Kurt. *Interpersonal communication*. New York: Pergamon Press, 1976.

Although the whole book deserves attention by the serious student of counseling, for the purposes of this chapter the reader is directed to Danzinger's thorough coverage of nonverbal communication channels in Chapter Four.

Ekman, Paul and Friese, Wallace V. Nonverbal leakage and clues to description, in *Psychiatry*, 1969, *32*, 88-106.

This article discusses the concept of leakage and the factors which contribute to validity as a source of information in the counseling session. In spite of our efforts to hide our emotions, leakage occurs in quite predictable ways.

Fast, Julian. *Body language*. New York: M. Evans and Co., 1970.

This is a popular source of information on nonverbal communication as long as it is not taken too literally.

Mehrabian, A. A semantic space for nonverbal behavior, in *Journal of Consulting and Clinical Psychology* (1970a) *35*, 248-257.

Mehrabian, A. When are feelings communicated inconsistently? in *Journal of Experimental Research in Personality*, 1970b, *4*, 198-212.

Mehrabian, A. and Wiener, M. Decoding of inconsistent communications, in *Journal of Personality and Social Psychology*, 1967, *6*, 109-114.

Mehrabian, A. and Williams, M. Nonverbal concomitants of percieved and intended persuasiveness, in *Journal of Personality and Social Psychology*, 1969, *13*, 37-58.

The above four articles are most pertinent to the understanding of nonverbal communication channels, the effects of inconsistent messages and to the understanding of the concept of leakage. They provide a good introduction to Mehrabian's work in this area.

Wiener, M. and Mehrabian, A. *Language within language: Immediacy—A channel in verbal communication*. New York: Appleton-Century-Crofts, 1968.

Unfortunately this book is out-of-print, but it is available at most university libraries. The authors introduce the concept of immediacy: how much the response of one person matches the statement of another — that is, meets the demands of that statement. This book is a solid introduction to the field of psycholinguistics as it relates to counseling and to nonverbal aspects of communication.

6

Self-Disclosure

SELF-DISCLOSURE and MENTAL HEALTH

Self-disclosure is the process of verbally sharing parts of one's experience, values and emotions with another. Jourard (1964) believes that the ability to self-disclose is a significant attribute in positive mental health. Through the very act of disclosing, we increase our self-knowledge. Through disclosing one's self to another, a person is crystallizing and clarifying those experiences and emotions for one's self. As well we probably find that the other person's acceptance of our experiences and emotions helps us to be more accepting of those parts of ourselves that we heretofore have disclaimed. Therefore, self-disclosing serves two functions: One, it helps to clarify our own understanding of self; and, two, it helps us to feel more positive and accepting of ourselves.

Self-disclosure is not something we do easily. Societal expectations are very implicit in providing "taboos" on self-disclosing behaviors. For one thing, due to conditions of crowding in cities and the traditional American independent spirit (typified by the strong, silent cowboy) there is a tremendous emphasis on and respect for privacy. It is not considered polite to inquire too deeply into someone's personal life, particularly in work settings and with that class of persons known as acquaintances. Even with close friends, privacy and "space" are valued and respected. We tend to quickly honor privacy even more, when our close friend's personal life is known to be in turmoil. The person who does not respect that privacy is described as nosy, a busybody, a snoop and worse. Conversely, the person who self-discloses (shares his/her personal life) in inappropriate settings is thought to be lacking in social graces.

Living in cities tends to increase the need for privacy. It is not unusual to live in an apartment building in New York, Los Angeles or Chicago for several years and not know the names of the other tenants, much less anything personal about them. Obviously, this much emphasis on privacy can contribute enormously to loneliness and feeling isolated from others.

Much of what operates to inhibit mental health is this feeling of being cut off from others. Without the opportunity to bounce off of others, to check out our internal reactions to experience, our perceptions have a way of becoming more important than they really are. (The Catholic Church may have recognized this problem of an internal cauldron when it instigated the sacrament of confession — a formalized way for one individual to self-disclose to another.) Actions which are not self-disclosed tend to become exaggerated and layered with feelings of guilt, shame and remorse. Perceptions and experiences are thought of as unique (different), and sometimes the very process of believing you are different and that you think and feel differently than others can add to your sense of isolation.

We are still curious creatures, and one way to resolve the oppositional needs of curiosity and to have privacy is to "guess" about the personal lives of others. Unfortunately, this guessing only serves to complicate matters. Either we guess that everyone's experiences are different from our own, which adds to our sense of isolation and uniqueness or we err in the other direction — assuming that everyone feels exactly the same way we do; that we "know" how everyone feels. Erring in this direction, we compound our problems because in "knowing" how someone else feels we never feel the need to check out our guesses. Both ways of resolving our needs to understand others (curiosity) and our needs of privacy add to further isolation because communication does not take place.

So what happens to our internal life? In many ways we cut it off. Our emotions become a closet that we open only to shove more emotions into and then quickly close the door again. Because self-disclosure is not easy, perhaps believed to be unacceptable, our emotions become unacceptable too. The relationship between this and our reluctance to communicate our emotions is obvious. Our reluctance to communicate our emotions, already difficult by definition, is made by the factors operating to inhibit self-disclosure of any form. We may be discussing two sides of the same coin.

To fully understand the ramifications of this process, let's examine the inner life of a young man we shall call Dennis. Dennis as a young boy had very murderous impulses toward his mother. When Mom slapped his hands for pinching his little sister, Dennis imagined a purple dragon biting off her head. Enjoying this fantasy, he elaborated on it several times in his daydreams with increasingly vicious symbolism. In one fantasy the dragon set the mother on fire; in another the dragon beat the mother to death with his tail. With all of these fantasies, Dennis felt guilty — after all, no one *really* wants to murder one's mother. He neither verbalizes his fantasies to anyone else nor talks about the negative emotions he has. Instead, he puts them away in a box, like Pandora, and maybe even stops fantasizing because the content of his fantasies has frightened him.

During adolescence, he falls "in love" with an older boy and is perplexed and troubled by his homosexual feelings. These too are never shared – into Pandora's box they go. He may even deny the existence of those feelings so strongly that he becomes a teenager who constantly belittles other boys for their seemingly feminine behavior. These actions make him somewhat uneasy, but the feeling of uneasiness is never shared and instead is shoved into Pandora's box.

Dennis meets a pleasant, attractive girl during his first year of college. They marry and Dennis soon finds his new wife is pregnant. He drops out of school so he can support his family. While working in the automobile factory, on the assembly line, he finds he has several fantasies of flushing his new son down the toilet. Guess where this fantasy goes?

Each of these critical incidents in Dennis's life are "normal", yet the reaction to them can interfere with mental health. Burying (repressing) our problems and our emotions can distort the significance of those experiences to the point where we believe (and fear) that we are responding in "abnormal" ways. At the very least, the individual, like Dennis, learns to think of himself in negative ways, to value himself as less "good" than others.

The ROLE of SELF-DISCLOSURE in COUNSELING

Self-disclosure may well be the basic unit of behavior in counseling. Jourard (1964) asserts that the function of the counselor is to assist a person who is distressed in the process of self-disclosure. At the beginning of therapy, the client is probably much like Dennis – in a state of self-alienation, having few significant others, if any, to whom s/he has been able to disclose her/his inner life. Since our inner life, our sense of self, is validated and clarified through continual interaction with others, lack of interaction and lack of self-disclosure leads to lack of self-validation. Our Pandora's box may seem less and less a part of us and our "being" can become separated from what we "seem" to be to others. Dennis's antagonism to femininity in males is certainly separated from his own attachments as a youngster. He is not what he presents to others.

Facilitating the process of self-disclosure is a basic skill for counselors. Many of the listening (content) responses assist the process of self-disclosure in that they focus on expansion of the story. By maintaining an attentive stance, the counselor encourages the client to move from Level One, the words and compressed content of his/her experiences, to Level Two, the expression of feelings (primarily in indirect ways) *during* the elaboration of content. Through use of skills such as reflection of feeling, the client's disclosures are validated and the *action* of disclosure is reinforced. The client will continue to self-disclose, perhaps increasing in risk, with reinforcement for the process.

Taking a second look at one's life experiences and perceptions in the presence of another sometimes provides the impetus for changing the way one views those experiences. Other skills will be necessary for the counselor to use in assisting the individual in changing his/her "Gestalt," or world-view, but the process of self-disclosing is a necessary requisite to change. The kinds of responses that are made to the self-disclosures are critical. Again, the counselor's value as a presence lies in the ability to withhold the expected, social response and to give the unexpected, asocial response.

If our client *has* been sharing his/her experiences with others, which is not likely in view of all the social pressures and taboos on self-disclosing, s/he has probably received a wide variety of responses. The client has managed, through verbal and nonverbal cues, to elicit social responses (disbelief, pity, surprise, etc.). If our client has not been talking about it, then his/her responses are internal and highly expected. The client has *imagined* the horror, the disbelief, the pity, the surprise. It is fairly easy to see how the individual's own internal responses can act as cues through nonverbal behavior to elicit exactly those responses from others which the individual most dreads.

The counselor, by responding in other than expected ways to the self-disclosure, to the contents of Pandora's box, can provide a neutral environment where the individual has to revise his/her own internal responses. Thus the process of change has begun.

Self-disclosures vary tremendously in ease. It is much easier to disclose factual, content-oriented information than to disclose content which carries with it a high emotional component. For example, it may be relatively simple and nonthreatening for a woman to state she is divorced. Stating the reasons and sequence of events surrounding the divorce is less easy and finally, disclosing the emotional responses one has to the divorce and to the ex-husband is considerably more difficult. The anxiety accompanying self-disclosure can be very real. In a sense, when we choose to disclose these central aspects of our self, we are revealing those areas which we feel most unsure; for some of us it may seem as if we are giving weapons to the hearer that s/he may or may not choose to use. Since we grow up in a society where we are frequently punished for the way we behave, think and feel, and discouraged from sharing private aspects of self, our sense of trust in others is not well-developed. We learn to keep many, if not most, of our thoughts to ourselves and display a public, pleasant self which can operate smoothly in many situations. Our public self may be far removed from what we are actually feeling. As Jourard (1964) points out, after too much experience with our public self, "our disclosures reflect, not our spontaneous feelings, thoughts, and wishes, but rather pretended experience which will avoid punishment and win unearned approval. We say that we feel things we do not feel. We say that we did things we did not do. We say that we believe things we do not believe. We may say the individual has then sold his/her soul, his/her real self, in order to purchase popularity, his mother's affection, or a promotion in the firm." Disclosing what we really feel and experience may be close to impossible. Some of us do not know what we really feel and experience.

Certain factors operate to facilitate self-disclosure. We disclose to those few that we trust, to those who bear some perceived similarity to ourselves, perhaps on the basis of surface characteristics. Jourard has found that women disclose more to women; men to men; adolescents to their peers. And frequently, when access routes to others seem to be closed, we disclose to a counselor. Jourard believes we cannot know our real selves except as a consequence of disclosing to another, and that the very act of disclosure strengthens our selves and is perhaps what therapy and counseling are all about. The client who tells the counselor that s/he has told him/her more than s/he has ever told another living soul *and feels good about it* is not unique.

Disclosure takes courage, and it takes time. Providing an atmosphere where disclosure is permissible and not at the counselor's discretion but at the client's is a difficult task. Disclosure also takes practice for most of us. Moving from Level One, content, to the second level where we can share the feelings associated with that content is not the typical mode of interaction. The example of the divorce, the reasons, and the emotions represent levels of experience *within* each of us and differing degrees of difficulty in self-disclosure.

One of the obvious benefits the counselor gains from being an effective facilitator of self-disclosure is that it reduces the counselor's need to "guess". True empathy is contingent on accurate listening and avoiding the pitfall of imagining – just as some of our clients do – that everyone feels exactly the same way we do. Too often in counseling, we obtain a little information and jump to immediate conclusions about how the client feels about that information. True empathy is not guesswork or jumping to conclusions. Jourard tells us that a more effective way of obtaining accurate concepts of a person's experiencing is to hear what that person is thinking and feeling. If our client has told us honestly (and by not giving him/her *our* cues so that s/he will revise the telling to please us or make him/herself more presentable we facilitate honest self-disclosure) we have the basis for perfect empathy: the client's own experiencing.

One of the best ways to facilitate self-disclosure in others is for the counselor to engage in brief self-disclosures. At a basic level, a room full of strangers will sit in silence until one person introduces him/herself, the simplest form of self-disclosure. The other members of the room will generally follow suit. There are several points in the counseling relationship where brief relevant self-disclosures by the counselor will assist the hesitant or "stuck" client in continuing in his/her process and flow of self-disclosure.

Example: Client: I don't know where to begin. I love my baby but I've felt so awful since he was born.

Counselor: I think I know what you mean. I remember that time after the birth of my child as extremely difficult.

Purpose: To facilitate at this point and to indicate understanding. The self-disclosure should be brief and return the focus immediately back to the client.

ACTIVITIES in SELF-DISCLOSURE

The activities for this chapter depart somewhat from our usual procedures. They are exercises in disclosure and are designed to help us recognize differing levels of communication, as well as to provide in the skill of self-sharing. Recognizing and describing feeling states in ourselves may not directly transfer to recognition and description of feeling states in others, but they tend to facilitate toward the direction of increased understanding.

Activities

1. Sit with your group in a comfortable arrangement. Describe an experience you had in which you felt *disappointment* totally in a content way, that is, describe objectively what happened. Then describe the feelings that you had when you went through this experience. Do not worry about being interviewed or interviewing others. Take turns in doing this exercise, not interrupting or commenting until the person has completed his/her description. Discuss each experience as a group after each person has completed both descriptions. Thus the sequence should go something like this:

content disclosure, feeling disclosure, group discussion, content disclosure, feeling disclosure, group discussion and so on around the group.

2.   Repeat, describing an experience in which you felt *anger*. Remember to separate content (the objective behavioral description) from feeling (what you experienced at the time).

3.   Discuss with your group any perceived differences in anxiety level between the two levels of description. Discuss any perceived levels of communication during this exercise.

4.   Share your perception of the exercise with the instructor.

5.   Tape the entire group activity.

* * * * *

SUGGESTED ADDITIONAL READINGS

Chelune, Gordon, J. Disclosure flexibility and social-situational perceptions, in *Journal of Consulting and Clinical Psychology*, 1977, *45*, 6, 1139-1143.

Chelune's research indicates that self-disclosure may have a curvilinear relationship to mental health and that the appropriateness of self-disclosure may be related to the ability to pick up situational norms and environmental cues governing appropriateness.

Cozby, P. Self-disclosure: A literature review, in *Psychological Bulletin*, 1973, *79*, 73-91.

This is a good source for summarizing the recent literature on self-disclosure and its relationship to mental health.

Doster, Joseph and Brooks, Samuel J. Interviewer disclosure modeling, information revealed, and interviewer verbal behavior, in *Journal of Consulting and Clinical Psychology*, 1974, *42*, 3, 420-426.

These investigators found that self-disclosure both which reflected favorably and unfavorably on the interviewer enhanced the amount of and quality of interviewee self-exploration as opposed to absence of interviewer self-disclosures.

Ellsworth, Robert B. Feedback: Asset or liability in improving treatment effectiveness? *Journal of Consulting and Clinical Psychology*, 1973, *40*, 3, 383-393.

Feedback, the process of sharing therapist perceptions with the client, is probably related to willingness to self-disclose. Ellsworth presents some of the conditions under which feedback has been found to be effective.

Jourard, Sidney M. *The transparent self.* New York: Van Nostrand Co., 1964.

This is the basic theory of the relationship of self-disclosure to mental health. It is excellent reading for anyone who plans on counseling as a career choice.

Kopfstein, Joan Held and Kopfstein, Donald. Correlates of self-disclosure in college students, in *Journal of Consulting and Clinical Psychology*, 1973, *41*, 163-168.

The researchers in this study focused on the interaction of the need for approval and sex with the ability to self-disclose. Both correlates were found to be related.

Luft, Joseph. *Group processes.* Palo Alto: Mayfield Publishing Co, 1970.

Luft presents his model of the Johari Window, an interesting schematic representation which can be applied to self-disclosure.

Simonson, Norman R. and Bahr, Susan. Self-disclosure by the professional and paraprofessional therapist, in *Journal of Consulting and Clinical Psychology*, 1974, 42, 359-363.

Simonson has found that there are restrictions on the amount and type of self-disclosures which are facilitating in therapy. The implications for the roles of professional and paraprofessional are discussed herein.

Unless you write in large letters, how else can I know you?

— Clark Moustakas

7

Self-Disclosure and Open Expression

Since self-disclosure is such a basic unit of behavior in the counseling interview, it seems prudent to examine in some detail the kinds of client disclosures which are most frequently *heard* and the various dimensions which determine the ease or difficulty of those disclosures.

The CONTENT AREAS of SELF-DISCLOSURE

Jourard and others (1964) have found content areas which were amenable to self-disclosure in varying degrees. These aspects of self can be grouped into six categories: attitudes and opinions, tastes and interests, work, money, personality (including past and present behavior), and the body. Subjects used in his research studies varied by sex, race, age and occupation on the amount disclosed in these areas and to whom they would disclose. Adolescents, for example, may find it easy to discuss their opinions (on most any given topic, much to the chagrin of some of the adults in their lives) and extremely difficult to discuss their personal appearance (the body). For many adolescent girls and boys, the mention of their acne or their weight is enough to cause an emotional outburst, seemingly out of proportion to the intended "innocence" of the comment. Those areas are simply off-limits. A young child — also to the frequent embarrassment of the adults in his/her life — will disclose anything.

We adults are much more selective about the content areas of our disclosure. It may be fairly easy for us to discuss the type of hobbies we have (tastes and interests) and extremely difficult to discuss our financial situation with an acquaintance, a same-sexed friend, a friend of the opposite sex, our spouse, our parent. Again, in a social gathering, where we exchange demographic and identifying information about ourselves, we disclose our name, where we work and perhaps the nature of our job, and we engage in discussions which probably reveal our attitudes and opinions; (such as political stance and what we think of the energy crisis). We may even indicate our passion for classical/modern/hard-rock music and our taste in movies. It is "inappropriate" to discuss our salary or our debts. Because it is "inappropriate", we feel uncomfortable doing so. This suggests dimensions of difficulty and ease, anxiety or fear associated with areas of the self.

EASE DIMENSIONS of SELF-DISCLOSURES

A. *"Closeness"*.   The ease or difficulty of disclosure may be directly related to how "close" a content area is for the individual. Altman and Taylor (1973) suggest a layered view of the personality which supports this idea of closeness of a topic. They define personality as having a surface peripheral dimension, and proceeding inward through several layers to the fundamental core characteristics of the self.

1. At the surface, peripheral layer, are basic information items which have to do with biographical characteristics (age, sex, hometown, etc.).

2. Intermediate layers contain opinions and attitudes about ideas and issues, probably including tastes and interests.

3. The more central layers contain the core characteristics of personality — fears, self-concepts — idealized and realistic views of self as well as the good-me and bad-me feelings about self and perhaps the person's basic values.

It is suggested that there is a parallel here between these layers of the person and the levels of communication in counseling. Our content level (Level One) parallels peripheral data; our mixed level (Level Two) contains much of the intermediate layer of the personality. And the core characteristics of personality parallel our Level Three. Altman and Taylor may well be describing the internal self-communication system and we may be simply extending this to the communication system which occurs between people.

Altman and Taylor clarify some of the behavioral properties associated with their layered personality which seem relevant to interpersonal relationships, especially the counseling relationship.

> Proceeding inward, there is more of a one-to-many relationship between aspects of personality. The more central areas have a greater impact on peripheral areas and have more linkages to other aspects of personality. . . Thus it is possible to derive characteristics of *many* peripheral

properties from knowledge of a few or even *one* central property. . . shifts
in central layers would be expected to have more of an impact than changes
in peripheral areas. For example, change in one's basic trust in people
would be expected to have a greater impact throughout the total personality than shifts in attitude about an . . . election.

As one goes toward central layers, personality items vary from
common to unique and from high to low visibility. . . One's self-image and
self-concept are not usually made readily accessible to others and are
generally unique.

The greater the depth of a characteristic, the greater the probability
that it represents a vulnerable aspect of personality. . .

More "socially undesirable" characteristics are also hypothesized to
reside in central layers of personality. This does not necessarily include
only negative characteristics, but also those defined as socially forbidden
by a reference group, such as public demonstration of warmth and affection
among men.

More central aspects of personality involve positive and negative affective properties of the total self in all respects rather than as a person in
a specific situation. As reflected in the difference between the self-perceptions "I am satisfied with my performance on this test," and "I am satisfied with how intelligent I am, " the deeper the characteristic, the more it
involves the total personality (Altman and Taylor, 1973).

Contrast the layers of personality touched by the following
statements:

"I am concerned about the problem of communication in our
culture." (attitude, peripheral, general, distant from core properties –
Level One of communication)

"I had trouble communicating with my parents as a kid." (behavioral perception, probable association with feelings, intermediary
layer – Level Two of communication)

"I cannot communicate with my husband and it makes my marriage seem so lonely." (need, feeling, concern, expressed vulnerability,
central to core properties – probably Level Three of communication)

B. *Temporal*.   The latter can also be placed along a time
dimension ("then" and "now") while the first seems to exist outside
of temporal considerations. That is, I am concerned about communication in this culture; I've probably always, at least in my adult life,
had a vague concern about communication in our culture; and, unless
some genius develops a solution for all of our communication problems or I find some new cause to become vaguely concerned about, I
probably always will be concerned with communication in this culture.

The temporal dimension can have a significant influence on the
difficulty or ease of our self-disclosures. For most of us, what is
either in the distant past or in the distant future is not as meaningful
nor as tied to core characteristics of personality as what is happening

now. When an individual is thirty it is relatively simple and comfortable to discuss dreams for retirement; when that same individual
is sixty-four, retirement may be the most anxiety-provoking area in
his/her personal life. I can tell almost anyone my childhood ambitions
but the ambitions and dreams which I hold today are not easy to
share with anyone. Past and future are not as "close" as the present
moment. We are living the present moment, and for most of us it is
inextricably bound up with our core characteristics of personality —
how we feel about ourselves.

C. **Cognitive - Affective.** As a general rule, it is easier to discuss things (content) than feelings. Part of the reasons for this are
cultural: We are a nation of peoples who have been well-educated
in topical discussions rather than in sharing our feelings. This has
been discussed at considerable length in previous chapters and there
is support, too, for this dimension in the layered view of personality
itself. The core characteristics are themselves defined by, surrounded
by, and expressed by feelings.

D. **Finished - Unfinished.** Another dimension which apparently affects the ease of self-disclosure has to do with closure. What
is complete is not as linked to emotional centers as what is incomplete.
What is resolved is less likely to be tied to core characteristics as what
is unresolved. Studies of motivation have contributed to a theory of
behavior, the findings of which are that people seek to find closure
in their actions, in their perceptions, and in their relationships
with others. A suggestion I have frequently given to graduate students who have difficulty in regularly working on written papers
is to stop for an evening in the middle of a sentence. Our need for
closure will nag at us until the sentence is complete, and usually one
day of that kind of nagging pressure is all we can tolerate. We tend
to complete at least that sentence as soon as we can.* Need for
closure varies across individuals, being more intense in some of us
compulsive types and less intense in more "mellow" personality
types. However, it strongly affects the ease of self-disclosures. If
the individual who had trouble communicating with his/her parents
as a child *still* has trouble in the present, it will be more difficult for
him/her to disclose that item than the person who has resolved his/her
parent-child communication hassles. Unresolved probelms are more
closely related to core aspects of personality. Therefore, more psychological energies — which are central to the personality — are distributed

---

*This study technique — or prod to self-discipline — is not supported as far as I
know by any empirical evidence, but it has aided a few students as well as this
book's completion.

to and invested in incomplete or unresolved matters than distributed to those which are closed and no longer seem to demand our attention.

E. *Verbal - Nonverbal.* Verbal and nonverbal modes of communication are used in unison and while they are synchronized in communication, they frequently are not conveying the same message. Signals which are sent along with verbalizations often determine the outcome of interactions more than the words themselves. The young lady who says no to her boyfriend's advances while snuggling into his embrace is a rather clear example of the double message sent by two or more modes of communication. Bateson's theory of double-bind communication (1956) points to the effects of conflicting messages on the hearer. As a general rule, the individual who receives conflicting messages will regard the nonverbal cues as more valid than the verbalization. Thus, the child whose mother states, "Come here, darling, and give me a hug" while physically holding the child at a distance, quickly conveys to the youngster her distaste for hugging. The child may interpret this as a rejection, but in either case the verbalization has been invalidated. At the very least, the child is confused by the data s/he has received. Smith (1976) found that continual exposure to this extreme dichotomy of messages as well as some sort of directive not to leave the field (the source of the conflict) causes significant increases in anxiety and a reduction in adaptability of normal individuals. Thus, the confusion one feels when unable to interpret messages on the basis of nonverbal cues *or* verbalizations (or any communicative source where two messages are sent simultaneously) may have tremendous impact on this whole area of ease of self-disclosure. Is it possible that the client who engages in verbalizations while sending conflicting nonverbal cues also feels anxious? In addition, we have found in the training situation that students find it awkward (difficult) to discuss their own and others' nonverbal behavior and relatively simple to focus on their own and others' verbalizations. It is therefore suggested that nonverbal cues are also more directly tied to core characteristics. They may in fact be the access route utilized by the individual for intentional or unintentional leaking of core characteristics.

LEARNING the PROCESS of SELF-DISCLOSURE

A. *Separating Content from Affect.* In the communication of experience, both the cognitive (content) and affective (feeling) aspects must be present for understanding to occur. If too much emphasis is placed in the telling on the cognitive, objective expression of an event, the intellectualization of experience occurs, much in the manner of a storyteller who gets wrapped-up in his/her own syntax.

We may understand the details of an event but as listeners we have no way of knowing how the speaker feels, and we all too frequently "guess" at the feelings of another. We may base our guess on how we might have felt in the same situation — which can be erroneous from a slight to mammoth degree. Our speaker has clinically, objectively dissected his/her life experience and we, the listeners, are left to interpret or misinterpret its significance in terms of our own life experiences or some universal understanding of behavior. The event has lost its uniqueness.

On the other hand, if too much emphasis is placed on the affective, subjective expression of an event, the communication has then lost its universality, its ability to be shared with another. The uniqueness of the reaction to the event overrides its understanding and while sympathy may occur within the listener, understanding and empathy do not. Sometimes antipathy results from the inability to connect to the emotion expressed. An inability to relate, to identify with the emoting of the speaker is frequently the cue that the experience is not being communicated at any level of understanding to the listener and/or is too overwhelming to the listener because it represents a too-rapid drop in the exchange level of conversation.

I believe I experienced an example of this several years ago when I was a student in San Francisco. I was coming home from classes on a streetcar late at night. A man got on the streetcar carrying a rose. Apparently, he had been drinking but not to any objectionable level. He sat down behind the driver, directly opposite me, and began talking to the people on the streetcar about the rose in his hand.

"Have you guys ever stopped to think about how beautiful a rose is," he began. "And what do we do to it? We cut it from the vine and let it die in our hands." With that he began to weep, spinning the rose between his fingers. No one in the car responded; most averted their eyes and looked out the windows; some looked at the man in disgust. I was aware that something had happened to this man which may have seemed to him to be analogous to the rose he was holding, perhaps, but there was no way I could communicate with him about his concerns. All I felt was pity, which somehow removed me from his experience and anguish still further. I do recall trying to imagine what might have upset him and, as I was considerably young and romantic, I fantasized several interesting key events — probably none of which had any relationship to the truth.

Recently a television news reporter commented on the inability of the public to become aroused or concerned by the plight of those who are starving in India, Biafra and Honduras. The sorrow is too great, the misfortune too awesome and the public is overwhelmed and has withdrawn, rather than coming forward to help. Yet, the reporter went on, the explanation of one child's life (in this case, two little girls from Honduras) put in such a way as to enable the listening public to understand the reality (content) of that life as well as to identify with the difficulties (affective) will do more to rouse mass concern and action to assist than any other sort of public appeal. We simply cannot identify with too much subjective experience, particularly the emotions related to sorrow, death and grieving. Our response is to objectify — *to provide the necessary balance in our understanding to prevent us from being overwhelmed.*

Along these same lines, consider the impact of the death of John F. Kennedy on a nation used to many deaths. The cognitive and affective input into national public understanding were tremendously balanced and the nation was enabled to grieve. The response was so great as to puzzle historians and others who pride themselves on their objectivity.

Ruesch (1961) has also described one of the tasks of the counselor as being that of assisting the client to merge his/her experiences. In other words, too much emphasis on objectifying experience is as stultifying as being a totally inner-based, subjective personality. The subjective personality, one who can only see life through his/her lenses, can only see others in terms of how s/he is affected by them. The subjective personality somehow seems locked inside of his/her own experience and can neither communicate his/her inner world to another nor can receive or understand another's inner world.

In developing this balance between the content and feeling modes, it may be necessary to focus on each of them separately. In moving from peripheral to more central levels of communication, it may be necessary to consciously register these levels. As we have seen, the cognitive/affective dimension is inextricably related to levels of communication: By separating an experience into its content and feeling components, we may be increasing both our understanding of those components and the process of self-disclosure.

B.   ***Listening to the Process of Self-Disclosure.***

1.   *Recognition of content.*   Content levels of self-disclosure describe the event or the experience objectively. The speaker is able, through choice of words and descriptions to communicate experiences in such a way that it generalizes beyond the speaker. In this way the experience has universality, that is, aspects of it are readily understandable.

2.   *Recognition of feeling.*   Self-disclosures of feeling are, of course, tied to the experience, but the feelings an experience may arouse in an individual are unique to that individual. We may share

emotions which are universal across peoples, but aspects of our responses to events and experiences are unique. A building burning to the ground can arouse grief in the tenants, financial panic in the owner, irritation and pressure in a fireman, delight in a new architect, and a headache to the insurance adjuster. The circumstances (content) of our experience help to determine and define the uniqueness of the reaction (feeling).

3.   *Understanding leaking.* Most of us do not limit ourselves to one mode of communication and as we are describing events which can be closely related to core characteristics of personality, the emotion which is associated and the anxiety which may be related to describing the more central aspects of self may "leak" through. As we have seen, the most available channel for leaking — the communication of emotions — is the nonverbal mode of expression. During the expression of content even the most skilled intellectualizer will communicate some aspects of his/her feelings about his/her representation nonverbally.

C.   *The Safety Factor in Self-Disclosure.* The very nature of the situation which initiates self-disclosure — that of describing an experience in terms of its content — is the same one which permits individuals to disclose at their own rate. If the speaker does not feel s/he is being heard correctly or if the anxiety aroused by the topic is more than was anticipated, the speaker may elect to stay with the content level, thus not increasing his/her anxiety. This suggests some important considerations for the listener and the counselor. One, it is unwise to underestimate the importance of the content as it serves as the "testing ground" for the speaker. By dipping a toe in the water s/he finds the comfort level for him/her and determines the receptiveness of his/her listeners. Two, the listener — the counselor — can indicate his/her valuing of the speaker's content through attentive listening. Three, the dimensions of difficulty and ease such as time, closeness and completion contribute to the relative safety of a topic. And finally, the content of an experience helps to determine and define the uniqueness of the feeling.

In relating experiences having to do with disappointment and anger in previous exercises, it is apparent that skill is needed to adequately communicate the content (objective) and the feeling (subjective) components of experience. Those who described events strictly in terms of content were equally as removed from their listeners as those who described events strictly in terms of feelings. And saying, "I know how you felt," is not sufficient to bridge the gap in communication.

Self-disclosures, then, can be about many things and proceed from peripheral to central levels with the development of trust in one's listeners. The content/feeling dimension apparently has some value in enhancing communication and both aspects must be present for understanding to occur. Effective interaction may well be based on the clear communication of both content and feeling, on a balance between objective and subjective, on experiencing events and communicating that experience at many layers.

ACTIVITY

Repeat the listening arrangement of the last session with your small group. Relate an event in which you experienced *loss*, paying particular attention to the distinction between content and feeling levels. In the role of the listener, note whether the speaker makes the distinction, whether you understand the event and whether you can relate to the feelings expressed by the speaker. Do not interrupt the speaker. Attend to nonverbal cues on the part of the speaker. At the end of the speaker's self-disclosure at both communication levels, give feedback to the speaker as to your understanding of his/her experience and how you may have felt while listening to him/her. Later, think about which level of communication was most comfortable for you. Why? Which seems to be most comfortable for the speaker (other members of the group)? What cues do you have to support your hypotheses? Share your reactions to this exercise with other members of the group and the instructor. Taping the entire activity and reviewing it later will also help to increase your understanding of the process.

* * * * *

SUGGESTED ADDITIONAL READINGS

Allen, Thomas W. and Whitely, John M. *Dimensions of effective counseling.* Columbus: Charles E. Merrill Publishing C., 1968. Chapter Five.

This chapter summarizes about twenty years of research into the role of psychological openness in psychological theory and lends considerable support for Jourard's theories of self-disclosure.

Altman, Irwin and Taylor, Dalmas A. *Social penetration.* New York: Holt, Rinehart and Winston, Inc., 1973.

Altman and Taylor attempt to examine the factors which influence and arise during the process of movement in social relationships from acquaintances to friendship and beyond. This book is particularly helpful in understanding the counseling relationship.

Eisenberg, Sheldon and Delaney, Daniel J. *The counseling process.* Chicago: Rand McNally College Publishing Co., 1977.

This excellent, easy-to-read introductory text for counselors has case studies, activities, concrete examples and practical suggestions. Of particular merit is Chapter Three, which clarifies the process of counseling from a similar stance as this chapter, that is, depth of communication levels and self-disclosure.

Jourard, Sidney M. *The transparent self.* Princeton: Van Nostrand Co., 1964.

This text is the basic introduction of Jourard's concepts of self-disclosure.

Jourard, Sidney M. *Self-disclosure: An experimental analysis of the transparent self.* New York: John Wiley & Sons, 1971.

Jourard reports on the reciprocal nature of self-disclosure, its implications for therapists and some of the initial attempts at research in this area.

Luft, Joseph. *Of human interaction.* Palo Alto: Mayfield Publishing Co., 1969.

Luft introduces the model of the Johari Window, its relationship to interpersonal communication and discusses aspects of the power and risk of self-disclosure.

Panyard, Christine Marie. Self-disclosure between friends: A validity study, in *Journal of Counseling Psychology*, 1973, *20*, 66-68.

This particular study seems to validate the necessity for relationships wherein one can self-disclose. It also provides additional support for the Jourard measure, the Self-disclosure Questionnaire.

Ruesch, Jurgen. *Therapeutic communication.* New York: W. W. Norten, 1961.

The role of the counselor in aiding the client to balance and merge his experiences is discussed thoroughly. The entire book is an excellent source.

Smith, E. Kim. Effect of the double-bind communication on the anxiety level of normals, in *Journal of Abnormal Psychology*, 1976, *85*, 4, 356-363.

This is a carefully constructed experiment into the effects of the double-bind on normals. Smith's findings showed that normal subjects found it nearly impossible to adapt to the situation and anxiety was increased.

PART III: Core Aspects of Personality

8

Understanding a Core Experience: Loss

Some years ago when I was selecting topics for my students to utilize in practicing self-disclosure, I chanced upon the topic of loss. Since that time several hundred students in my classes have reacted to the "loss tape" as the most significant learning in the course. Initially, the reaction surprised me. Later, it became apparent to me that the "loss tape" triggered several important responses. First, for many students it became the first opportunity they ever had to work through their feelings associated with early losses. Second, the cognitive/affective dimensions seemed particularly well-suited (and well-exemplified by) the individual styles of coping with loss. Third, loss had a strangely haunting quality for me and for my students: It was universally shared yet rarely talked about. Fourth, loss is the more generalized experience of death and bereavement, a topic which is strongly returning to the center of campus attention. This impetus in society had side benefits for training in counseling. And fifth, the salient importance of the counselor-as-listener was brought home with impressive clarity, sometimes with tenderness and sometimes painfully.

GROWING INTEREST in LOSS, SEPARATION, DEATH — DYING

During this century we have witnessed a remarkable disappearance of dying from our lives. Medicine has made advances against all kinds of diseases and more and more children have a chance of surviving infancy and progressing to a ripe old age. An infant born today can reasonably expect (if infants care about such things) to live well into his/her seventies. At the same time, deaths which used to occur naturally in the home (through illness, old age, etc.) have been removed from our vision — to the confines of a hospital or a nursing home. It is not unusual at all to be advised over the telephone that the significant people in our lives have died. Our contact with the dying has gone from fairly common, in the natural order of things, to minimal contact — the unnatural order. Thus when Simone de Beauvoir says, *There is no such thing as a natural death. Nothing that happens to a man is ever natural, since his presence calls the world into question. All men must die: but for every man his death is an accident and, even if he knows it and consents to it, an unjustifiable violation*, we of the twentieth century know exactly what she means. Dying is unexpected, inappropriate, physically distant and disconcerting.

There is a difference between dying and death. While we have managed to remove observation of the process of dying from our lives, we have also come face-to-face with the concept of macro-death (Elliot, 1972). We do not kill people one-at-a-time anymore; we exterminate them in huge numbers. The twentieth century may be unique because of its invention of so many creative methods of extermination. Elliot (1972), in discussing these "death-machines" has counted over 110 million people who have been killed by government action since 1900. Wars used to be personal encounters, man-to-man squabbling over boundary lines, water rights, power, etc. Now we have the ludicrous (and frightening) situation of two or more nuclear warheads, two death-machines facing each other. Massive destruction of non-combatant populations (non-soldiers) is the potential outcome. *The ultimate threat posed by nuclear weapons is not only death but meaninglessness: an unknown death by an unimaginable weapon* (Lifton, 1976).

A young veteran of Vietnam made the following comment about his experiences as a soldier, *Recapitulations of my perceptions of death . . . death of others and death of self . . . announced a mutation of my personality: I was becoming impervious to the death of my fellow soldiers, and, in addition, I was negating the possibility of my own possible demise* (Baruch, 1972). The indifference he began to feel is strangely reminiscent of the death-apathy described by Bendikson (1976). It may be that the two forces have caused a parallel reaction. Because our experience with dying is so limited (and our own death so unimaginable) and our experience with death so massive we have become apathetic and indifferent: *I'll think about that when the time comes.*

In the late 1950's a renewed interest in dying and the problems associated with death occurred. We have as yet, no explanation for this resurgence of interest. It may represent another attempt to deal with the age-old anxiety about death; it may be that the over-exposure to macro-death has brought death and its anxiety back into our awareness to the point where it had to be dealt with in some intellectualized way. It may be that with the emphasis on communication and relationships, the severance of relationships, of life itself, is no longer a taboo topic. It may also be that, as Gorer (1976) describes, death is our new pornography: We have worked out all of our hang-ups about sex, and we are ready to approach death, the other critical and puzzling fact of our existence (Freud, 1959). Unfortunately, it may be just a chic subject which will only serve to intellectualize our understanding of it and and obscure our acceptance of it as a basic fact of human experience (Weisman, 1977).

Along with the phenomenon of renewed interest in death and dying, there has been an increased awareness of the problems experienced by the survivors — the bereaved family and friends of the deceased. Research into the area of bereavement has indicated that how we respond to losses earlier in our history — that is, our background experience with loss, often determines our responses to bereavement.

LOSS as a MICROCOSM of COUNSELING CONCERNS

It may well be, because of the profound nature of the loss experience, that loss can provide an understanding of human responses in many stress situations. The range of responses an individual has to grief and loss includes every emotion of which a human is capable. Numbness and denial of the impact itself, guilt and remorse over incomplete relationships and feelings expressed or left unsaid, responsibility and avoidance of the additional burdens imposed by another, anger at the sense of abandonment, fear at facing loneliness and tremendous resistance to change — these are just a sample of the normal range of emotions experienced by the one who loses. The expression "rupture of loss," used by Parkes (1972) expresses the wrenching sense that something which once felt complete to the individual has been pulled away, rupturing the place behind. The individual's identity is often dependent on the one-who-is-missing. Foreseeing a future where we have to visualize ourselves without that one-who-is-missing is tremendously difficult. The one who has lost resents and resists the changes in self-perception, the changes in life style, the changes created by daily absence.

Developing a depth of understanding about the process of loss has an implicit coordinate. To experience loss one must have developed some sense of attachment. Thus, loss most clearly exemplifies the interrelatedness of emotions. Every attachment has some built-in loss potential. *The pain of grief is just as much a part of life as the joy of love; it is, perhaps, the price we pay for love* (Parkes, 1972). How much this risk potential influences us is evidenced by our willingness to enter into relationships. Fear of abandonment and fear of loss, often prevent many of us from trusting our relationships with others, or even from entering into new relationships with others. Love, commitment, trust and attachment (perhaps) can be balanced on one side against the difficulties associated with loss, grief and aloneness on the other. Loss can help increase our understanding of attachment and the strength of the bond between individuals and the resistance to severing that bond (Parkes, 1972).

Losses obviously are not limited to people. Any tangible or intangible thing which is seen as part of one's identity can be attached to and similarly lost. It is not too difficult to understand those who ended their lives with the stock market crash during 1929, unable to accept the change in self-identity which accompanied financial loss. For some of us, remembering the sense of loss we had as children when a favorite toy disappeared or a pet disappeared from our lives, can clarify this attachment/loss process. Our relationship to loss and attachment may well be the central life experience.

LOSS as a CORE EXPERIENCE
Universally shared yet rarely discussed — the avoided issue

Psychologists are just beginning to examine the role loss plays in development of an individual from infancy to old age. The central nature of loss has been carefully delineated by Kastenbaum and Aisenberg (1972). It is their premise that a child begins to develop concepts of death and loss through experiencing separation from its mother. Because mother is conceived of as part of the child in earliest infancy (i.e., the infant's identity is dependent on this mothering person) and because the child has not yet developed any conception of future time, the absence of the mother is perceived as loss, a kind of practice death. That is, the separation of the mothering parent from the child *before* the child has developed a sense of *me* and *not me* is experienced as disappearance of self, *partial loss of the individual.* At the same time, they note that *we cannot experience the disappearance of an object unless we have already acknowledged its existence as a relatively enduring entity* (Kastenbaum and Aisenberg, 1972). The relationship of loss to developing attachments is thus emphasized.

Many of the separations and object-losses experienced by the infant and young child are trivial and unimportant to our adult retrospective vision, yet Kastenbaum and Aisenberg suggest that in principle each time these separations and losses occur the child experiences a sense of self-loss.

As the child matures, its attachments to others increase. From the basic family unit the child extends her/his relationships to school teachers, peers and other representatives of society. Concurrently with this widening circle of attachments, the child develops a stronger sense of self, of ego, and the increased ability to recognize people and other objects as constant in his/her life. Carr (1975) points out that the likelihood for exposure to separation and loss increases, too.

Parkes (1972), Carr (1975) and Kastenbaum and Aisenberg (1972) all agree that with the increased ability to develop warm and satisfying attachments one also increases one's vulnerability to feelings of loss, sadness and grief when those attachments are disrupted.

The adolescent, because his/her ego strength is somewhat weakened by the struggle to crystallize his/her identity, is highly sensitive to loss and to death. What is perceived as necessary to one's identity is particularly susceptible to feelings of separation and loss. The ending of a romance during adolescence may well be one of life's severest blows because the romance is inextricably bound up with conceptions (often idealized) of self.

Throughout our maturing years *we are continually subjected to separations and losses which are so subtle or so well disguised that they may never be recognized or acknowledged . . . we are confronted with and tested by loss and separation throughout life . . .* (Carr, 1975). Kastenbaum describes these psychic "emotional" losses as *partial deaths* (Feifel, 1977).

Cassem (1975) contends that many of these losses are indispensable for growth. If we re-examine the child's attachment to its mothering parent, it becomes immediately apparent that in order for growth to occur that attachment must be ruptured. Hopefully, it is ruptured at a time when the child is ready for it, ready to integrate and recover from the break, but in any event it must occur. The child-becoming-adult cannot have his/her personal identity dependent on the attachment to and nurturance from the mother. Autonomy and growth are inseparable.

In a similar vein, revision of personal goals, when necessary in young adulthood or in the mid-years of life, involves the relinquishing of some aspects of self and a sense of loss. Growth to other goals, to satisfaction and a sense of integrity are often dependent on the abandonment of the child-like, narcissistic attachments to views of an unattainable idealized self.

Cassem also maintains that the changes in functional abilities and physical appearance associated with the aging process involve a loss of a narcisstic view of self. If my identity is dependent upon my being able to run the half-mile track in three minutes then the loss of that ability due to declining bodily functions is going to be a loss as real and as painful as the loss of a beloved person. Sheehy (1976), in her remarkable book, *Passages*, points out developmental stages of adulthood which are, in fact, centered around the core experience of loss.

All of these experiences occur so naturally (and so painfully) for most of us that they are acknowledged only rarely to ourselves and almost never to others. This peculiar state of affairs is attributable to one of the basic premises of this text: We rarely disclose our inner feelings to others. Since thoughts of death, feelings of loss, involve our core responses they are "taboo" in our society. Other topics are more socially correct. Two grown men who are both experiencing feelings surrounding the loss of potency, the loss of idealized views of their career accomplishments, and the loss of their dependents into adulthood are far more likely to discuss the weather with each other. Thus loss becomes the avoided issue. If we believe with Lindemann (1976) that what is not dealt with is likely to cause problems, then many unresolved or unsettled instances of loss can be the basis for personal anxiety and discomfort around the attachment to another person; loss may well be the core concern of many of our clients.

The AFFECTIVE/COGNITIVE DIMENSIONS
of CORE EXPERIENCE — LOSS

As in every experience, we relate to loss on more than one level. The *fact* of loss has occurred and whether or not we attempt to deny the reality, intellectually and cognitively, we are aware of that fact. Loss does not just occur in a vacuum. There are circumstances leading up to the event, and there is a thing or a person who is lost. The basic how, when, what and who of the experience are generally readily available to us. Our emotions may only allow us to verbally and cognitively replay the events to others for a time after the loss. In cases of bereavement, the survivors often recount the events associated with the death in a very matter-of-fact way, almost business-like in their conversations for several hours (and often a few days) immediately following the death.

This cognitive reaction to loss is normal and is probably the organism's way of protecting itself until a certain amount of readiness has occurred. Freud (1959) called the rehashing of events leading up to the death, the anticipatory response to part of the process of *grief work*. Parkes (1972) clarifies the process:

> At such a time, there is a conscious need to *get it right*, and getting it right is not just a matter of recalling the traumatic event correctly; it includes the need to *make sense* of what has happened, to explain it, to classify it along with other comparable events, to make it fit one's expectations of the world . . . trying out new solutions, searching for clues to explain *why did it happen to me?* and repeatedly, monotonously, remembering the sequence.

This numbing phenomenon has been noted by several researchers (Lifton, 1977; Volkan, 1975 and White, 1977), and while the actual impact of the death or loss may be denied, the events seem to be accessible and may, in fact, aid the bereaved in denial until s/he is ready for acceptance of the impact. Adults utilize the denial that they need

White (1977), and it appears that there may be a secondary cognitive process which contributes to denial, particularly in the instance of loss-by-death. Death is a unique experience in that no one can really state that they have an understanding of it. We cannot conceptualize our own death because we cannot conceptualize not conceptualizing (Schneidman, 1976). We have all kinds of intellectual strategies for trying to cope with the existence of death (including intellectual interest in the subject and working with death and the dying), but our own death *is indeed unimaginable and whenever we make an attempt to imagine it we can perceive that we really survive as spectators. Hence the psychoanalytic school could venture on the assertion that at the bottom no one believes in his/her own death, or to put it another way, in the unconscious everyone of us is convinced of his/her own immortality* (Freud, 1959).

Yet when someone we love dies, our conviction is shaken, and we are face-to-face with the fact of death. Bluebond-Langner (1977), describes the reaction of children to hearing of someone's death. They relate it immediately to themselves because of what Kastenbaum and Aisenberg call the child's cognitive pendulum (1972). *He is dead* is replaced with *I am dead* and usually accompanied by some fear at the idea. It is my contention that this process is not unique to children. Children are just better at verbalizing their cognitive processes. In other words, many adults have the same thought when someone they know dies: *He is dead* is replaced with *I am dead*, which is the process of reminding us of our own mortality. An adult *progresses* to the next step: *He is dead* replaced with *I am dead* replaced with *He is dead*, hence, the sometimes noted relief that the other is the victim, not the self, and (probably) some of the strongest feelings of guilt for thinking in this manner. Yet these thoughts are normal and are also part of the process of attempting to cognitively make sense out of both the event and death itself.

Many other forms of loss, besides death and bereavement, have cognitive processes which contribute to denial and numbing. This period of numbing usually follows the actual severance of ties and lasts for several hours. This is natural and a part of the psychological resistance to the event and a preliminary to accepting the events in reality in smaller, more palatable doses. As Parkes (1972) has noted, there is a time not to feel.

Guilt is one of the feelings associated with the loss event. One of the first feelings to emerge is pain at the rupture of loss. Thus begins the difficult phase − the actual grieving. (Because of the intense discomfort of this phase, many seek to avoid it, grasping tightly to the struggle to cognitively understand the reality of the event and persevering in the recounting of the events. With this kind of avoidance the experiencing of affect surrounding the loss is brief, recurring and somewhat undimensional.) Normal grieving includes a wide range of uncomfortable emotions: pain, bewilderment, anger — at life in general for its cruelty, at the specific people *responsible* for the loss and at the lost one for abandoning, — guilt for any positive emotions which might occur at this time (How could I feel this way when . . . ?), guilt at all the unsaid and undone things in the relationship and guilt at all the real and imagined hurts that normally occur in every relationship. And, again, normal grieving occurs at losses which occur through death or any other means. The range of feelings at *any* loss is extraordinary. People have differing ways of reacting to their losses and different ways of expressing their feelings. Some will cry and sob, some will be angry and berate those around them and life in general for its cruelty, and some will reveal their feelings in other ways. Some fear losing control and feel their grasp on reality is slipping. The important thing is for feelings to be permitted; how they are expressed is of secondary importance. Any act which inhibits the expression of appropriate grief is only making grief work more complex. These reactions and fears are in fact normal, if frequency of occurrence is any indication, and are far more healthy than the absence of grief (Parkes, 1972). *Grief may be seen as nature's exercise in loss and restitution. It involves pain but it is normally worked through and ultimately resolved* (Volkan, 1975). Loss, through experiencing and integration, can often deepen our experience and understanding of life and can truly be *a crisis to grow on*.

The COUNSELOR and LOSS

There is a very basic rationale for our attempting to understand the process of loss. Every counselor should have at least a moderate understanding of the way his/her own emotions respond to stress, of the nature of attachment and of the potential severance clients, and yet each counseling relationship has a built-in loss in the process of termination. An analogy can be drawn to Cassem's discussion of parent-child relationships: They must be severed for growth to occur. How well we, as counselors, cope with loss may well determine the strength of the attachments we form; if we cannot tolerate the thought of loss we may bind our clients too closely to us or not attach to them at all, hiding behind the *professional* distance which is necessary but not sufficient for productive counseling relationships.

Over and over again in the literature on loss and bereavement and from my own experience there is a basic tenet for counselors who would work with the loss and pain in others: It is wise to have one's own feelings about loss and bereavement at some kind of comfortable resolution. If a client has avoided the discomfort associated with grief it will be totally counter-productive for him/her to begin exploring his/her feelings with a counselor who is him/herself uncomfortable. The anxiety that is aroused in the unwary counselor is considerable and can only serve to reinforce in the client that, in fact, these feelings *are* overwhelming and inappropriate. Weisman (1977) points out the heavy demands that are placed on the counselor or therapist who is helping in the grief process:

> . . . *the patient may make severe demands upon the therapist. These demands are such that the therapist is asked to surrender part of his or her own autonomy and reality, to bolster the narcissism and diminish the deprivations that a patient has endured.*

And Weisman, also supports the developmental nature of the loss construct when he states, *Frequently these deprivations derive from earlier losses and deaths of significant others.* The stress that is placed on a counselor is considerable; when the counselor is uncertain and/or uneasy about loss and one of its specific agents, death, the amount of assistance that can be genuinely given is minimal.

> *As a prerequisite for asking patients to confront mortality, I have advised professionals first to confront their own* (Weisman, 1977).

Oddly enough, it is the very act of developing an interest in loss and death and dying that frequently spurs professionals into this area as a specialization.

> *Most of us seek out helping professions, at least partly, to meet such needs of our own as wanting to feel useful and important to others and to prove to ourselves that we can understand and cope with emotions, especially our own. As many of us come to terms with our own fears – particularly those related to death and dying – and feel that we have overcome them, we may be so eager to put our accomplishments to the test that we rush in without being truly needed as primary support givers* (Lyall and Vachon, 1975).

One of the best internal clues a counselor has that he or she is operating from own needs or unresolved fear masquerading as zealous eagerness to help is what Lyall and Vachon (1975) allude to above: making the choice to become the primary support giver. In every client's life there are those significant others who could learn to be supportive at this critical time. In the case of death, the professional has a particular responsibility to provide the kinds of interventions which will permit the bereaved members of a family to develop a therapeutic support system for each other. An effective counselor is not necessarily Wonder Woman or the Lone Ranger. Many of the counselor's duties will involve the orientation of significant persons in the client's life to optimal assistance of the process.

The SPECIALIZED SKILL

It is important to underline the fact that a counselor's role in assisting clients to deal with loss and grief will be tempered or enhanced by his/her own emotional reactions to such crises. As with other kinds of problems, the best teacher of these emotional reactions is experience. Gradually one learns to pace oneself *with* the client, to tune in during the cognitive recital and to facilitate the affective working-through.   Immediately after loss has occurred, assistance should be given with simplest decisions during the period of numbness, providing lots of time and company who can talk *about* the lost person without too much of their own discomfort getting in their way. The counselor's role is that of listener, gaining as much information as possible as to the place the lost person held in the bereaved's life. Neither probing nor jollying along help the client. The point is to be there and to listen.

The moment to move into the level of feelings is one that has to be a kind of intuitive, gradual step, unless of course the client takes the lead.   The process of working through the many emotions is tedious and draining for the counselor. Those who try to rush the process or to encourage a client to stop grieving before he or she is ready to do so may be surprised at the client's indignant reaction (Parkes, 1972).   Grief work, recovery, cannot be rushed, for the greatest threat to the client throughout the process is the actual acceptance of the loss as a reality. As long as the client is grieving or responding to the lost one, he or she is containing the rupture and keeping the lost one as part of the client's life until readiness has developed physically and mentally to accept that reality, the reality that the lost one *is* lost.

If the client seems stuck at the emotional level, or one-dimensional in the presented affect, it may be wise to back-track to the cognitive processing again.   Recounting the actual incidents surrounding the death or the separation is helpful because in addition to being a rehearsal for accepting the reality of the loss, the separation itself provides a great many clues as to unresolved emotions around the event. This is frequently a clue that one of the emotions being unexpressed is dominating the response and the client is struggling for containment. Reviewing the *history* can frequently provide the missing information which can trigger the underlying affect.

Persevering on a core experience for a client occurs when some aspect of the experience is not dealt with. At the same time, the counselor should be aware that the period of mourning following the death of a loved one lasts for a period of six months to a year. Grief following other losses may also be time-consuming. The after effects of divorce can extend to three years. Again, in Parkes' view, there is a time not to feel, a time to grieve, a time to mourn the loss and a time to begin anew.

All of the basic skills which have been presented are helpful in dealing with core experiences, In this arena, the counselor pays less attention to the social reinforcers which may be perpetuating the response and more attention to the missing data.

Understanding the loss experiences, which may well be the key life crises in all our lives, has much to teach the potential counselor about the experiencing and witnessing of pain and strength in our clients and in our own lives. That loss can provide impetus for tremendous growth is apparent; that it can also be the foundation for pathology, unresolved heartache and psychological problems is equally obvious. It is my contention that some aspect of loss is involved in every growth process, and, with Cassem, I believe there is a need to mourn the outgrown child in all of us as we move on to fuller integration of life's experiences.

ACTIVITIES

1.   In thinking about the experience of loss it is sometimes helpful to personalize its meaning. *Epitaphs* is one way to do this. In your small group discuss what you would like on your imaginary epitaph.   To whom would your message be directed?   What does it express about the meaning of your life?

2.   Poll your group to find out which members and how many prefer the traditional funeral and burial ceremonies. What alternatives are there?   What are some of the reasons people might select alternatives to burial? Personalize your discussion as much as possible.   Be aware of the ease/difficulty of this topic and of nonverbal concomitants of the discussion.

3.   Extend the previous discussion into imagining your own idealized (preferred) death.   Contrast your preferences with the statistical findings that most adults die in the hospital or in institutionalized settings (nursing homes).

4. Tape the entire activity and review it after you have finished. What nonverbal behavior did you notice? Was member participation good? Where would you place the discussion on a cognitive/affective dimension? Where would you place your participation on a cognitive/affective dimension? Did members listen to each other? How supportive were you of divergent opinions?

* * * * *

SUGGESTED ADDITIONAL READINGS

Baruch, Joel. Combat death. In Edwin S. Schneidman (Ed.), *Death: Current perspectives*. Palo Alto: Mayfield Publishing Co., 1976.

This sad article describes the development in a former Viet Nam soldier of indifference to death and a growing belief in his own invulnerability. Perhaps the two are related.

Bendikson, Robert. The sociology of death. In Robert Fulton (Ed.), *Death and identity*. Bowie, Md.: Charles Press Publishers, Inc., 1976.

This is a solid introductory article to the western views of death and their impact on a culture and identity. It is difficult reading, but worth the effort.

Bluebond-Langner, Myra. Meaning of death to children. In Herman Feifel (Ed.), *New meanings of death*. New York: McGraw-Hill, 1977.

The author contrasts the views of normal children with the views of terminally ill children and draws some conclusions about the unique meanings death concepts have for children — which may or may not be that unique to children.

Carr, Arthur C. Bereavement as a relative experience. In Bernard Schoenberg et al. (Ed.). *Bereavement: Its psychological aspects*. New York: Columbia University Press, 1975.

Carr introduces the thesis that life consists of one separation-loss experience after another and that we are continually tested by these experiences. Carr seems to be stressing the *normalcy* of loss and separation.

Cassem, Ned H. Bereavement as indispensable for growth. In Bernard Schoenberg et al. (Ed.). *Bereavement: Its psychological aspects*. New York: Columbia University Press, 1975.

Along with the contention that separation and loss are normal activities, (See Carr.) Cassem makes a convincing argument for the necessity of certain losses and separations for healthy development. An example of this is in the young adult separating from his family to be independent. It is an excellent, thought-provoking article.

de Beauvoir, Simone. *A very easy death*. New York: Putnam and Sons, 1966.

This author had a very difficult relationship with her mother throughout her life. The book chronicles her mother's illness and death, and its affects on their relationship. It is poetically written.

Elliot, Gil. *The twentieth century book of the dead*. New York: Ballantine Books, 1972.

This book describes the concept of megadeath and chronicles the 110 million people who have been killed by government action in this century. Although it sounds depressing, it is not. The book is brilliant satire, and it leaves the reader angry and intrigued by historical "ethics."

Feifel, Herman. Attitudes toward death: A psychological perspective. In Edwin S. Schneidman (Ed.), *Death: Current perspectives*. Palo Alto: Mayfield Publishing Co., 1976.

Feifel discusses the impact death-as-a-future-event has on the individual in the present. He elaborates on some of the resources used to cope with the idea of dying.

Feifel, Herman (Ed.). *New meanings of death*. New York: McGraw-Hill, 1977.

This collection of nineteen articles is aimed at the college student and includes a wide variety of topics, from clinical management of the dying, to helping the bereaved, to the the roles of funerals.

Freud, Sigmund. Thoughts for the times on war and death. In *Collected papers*, vol. 4. New York: Basic Books, 1959, 288-317.

This is late-vintage Freud and should be savored with his psychoanalytic approach in mind and with an openness to provocative, intriguing writing. It provides good background material.

Fulton, Robert (Ed.). *Death and identity*. Bowie, Md.: Charles Press Publishers, 1976.

This book is a collection of twenty-seven articles on the various aspects of death and dying — theoretical, attitudinal, reactional. It includes articles on anticipatory grief and funerals, as well as reports of investigations into the reactions of specific populations to grief.

Gorer, Geoffrey. The pornography of death. In Edwin S. Schneidman (Ed.), *Death: Current perspectives*. Palo Alto: Mayfield Publishing Co., 1976.

Gorer's thesis is that death is now the taboo subject that sex once was during the Victorian Age. He carries the analogy through this article and discusses the inhibition of death-ideas in children and in adults. Gorer also contends that the emotions associated with both of these topics are paid little or no attention.

Kastenbaum, Robert and Aisenberg, Ruth. *The psychology of death*. New York: Springer Publishers, 1972.

This is an outstanding reference work which attempts to trace the development of conceptualizations about death from infancy to old age with its concomitant impact on the personality. It is strongly recommended to the counselor who plans to work in this specialty.

Kubler-Ross, Elizabeth. *On death and dying*. New York: Macmillan Publishing Co., 1969.

This is probably the most widely recognized book on this topic. Kubler-Ross provides a good introduction to the taboo topic and includes many personal vignettes.

Levinson, Peritz. Obstacles in the treatment of dying patients, in *American Journal of Psychiatry*, 1975, *132*, 1, 28-32.

This is an informative article wherein the author acknowledges the tremendous growth of interest in the field yet maintains that those who need the services most are still not getting them. Case histories and recommendations are included.

Lifton, Robert J. and Olson, Eric. The nuclear age. In Edwin S. Schneidman (Ed.), *Death: Current perspectives*. Palo Alto: Mayfield Publishing Co., 1976.

Lifton and Olson contend that the effects of nuclear threat have considerably changed our views of potential loss, separation and death. Presented here are several interesting modes for dealing with the urge for immortality. This article is vital as a backdrop for the entire understanding of our renewed interest in death and loss.

Lifton, Robert J. The sense of immortatlity. In Herman Feifel (Ed.), *New meanings for death*. New York: McGraw-Hill, 1977.

Although it is difficult reading, this article expands many of the modes of dealing with the urge for immortality discussed in the Lifton and Olson article and also discusses the practical application of these ideas in counseling.

Lindemann, Erich. Symptomatology and management of acute grief. In Robert Fulton (Ed.). *Death and identity*. Bowie, Md.: Charles Press Publishers, Inc., 1976.

Although this is the pioneer work which first clearly delineated the grief syndrome, it is still applicable.

Lyall, Alan and Vachon, Mary. Professional roles in thanatology. In Bernard Schoenberg et al. (Ed.), *Bereavement: Its psychological aspects*. New York: Columbia University Press, 1975.

A valid article that should be read by anyone considering this area as a specialty. The authors caution the counselor against overactive and intrusive intervention, and raise some very good points in the process.

Parkes, Colin Murray. *Bereavement*. New York: International University Press, 1972.

This well-written book is an invaluable source which deals with many aspects of loss, including its generalization to many life-experiences and gives suggestions for effective, professional dealing with the bereaved client.

Schneidman, Edwin S. (Ed.). *Death: Current perspectives*. Palo Alto: Mayfield Publishing Co., 1976.

This is one of the most thorough accounts of the current compilations on death. Schneidman's book is well-organized and has the additional advantage of introductions to each section by Schneidman. All of these are well-written and can stand alone as valuable contributions. Note particularly the introductions to numbers five, six and seven and the articles by Schneidman on postvention and death-work.

Schoenberg, Bernard et al. (Ed.). *Bereavement: Its psychological aspects*. New York: Columbia University Press, 1975.

This book of readings is of general interest on the subject of loss, its developmental history and its ramifications for professionals.

Scott, Frances G. and Toobert, Saul. Death and dying: An approach to training professionals. In A. Schwartz and I. N. Mensch (Ed.), *Professional obligations and approaches to the aged*. New York: Charles C. Thomas, in press.

Some of the ideas included in this article can be adapted by the individual who is interested in working with loss and bereavement, in that they can be used for self-understanding and increasing one's awareness of the problems inherent in the topic.

Sheehy, Gail. *Passages*. New York: E. P. Dutton and Co., 1976.

This monumental best-seller attempts to extend the developmental life-crises of Erikson to adult normal development and, as such, deals in larger measure with the concepts of separation and loss. The first several chapters are particularly recommended.

Smith, Joseph H. On the work of mourning. In Bernard Schoenberg et al. (Ed.), *Bereavement: Its psychosocial aspects*. New York: Columbia University Press, 1975.

This interesting article discusses the historical components of any major adult loss.

Vecors, J. *Sylva*. New York: Macmillan, 1964.

This is fiction but its value in transmitting an understanding of the place of death in our personality development is immeasurable.

Volkan, Vamik D. Re-grief therapy. In Bernard Schoenberg et al. (Ed.), *Bereavement: Its Psychosocial aspects*. New York: Columbia University Press, 1975.

This article details one therapist's approach to counseling the bereaved. There are some useful suggestions. Balance this one with the Lyall and Vachon article.

Weisman, Avery D. Denial and middle knowledge. In Edwin S. Schneidman (Ed.), *Death: Current perspectives*. Palo Alto: Mayfield Publishing Co., 1976.

Weisman is one of the more eloquent writers in this field and this treatment of denial is invaluable. It also extends nicely to forms of denial other than death denial. It is must reading for the prospective thanatologist.

Weisman, Avery D. The psychiatrist and the inexorable. In Herman Feifel (Ed.), *New Meanings of death*. New York: McGraw-Hill, 1977.

Several issues are raised and discussed by this author and the article sums up the difficulties involved in working in this field. It is highly accurate and very readable.

Weisman, Avery D. Appropriate death. In Edwin S. Schneidman (Ed.). *Death: Current perspectives*. Palo Alto: Mayfield Publishing Co., 1976.

The value of this article lies in the concept of an "appropriate" death, which Weisman strongly advocates. He explains that for each individual the definition of an appropriate death is unique.

White, Laurens P. Death and the physician: Mortus vivos docent. In Herman Feifel (Ed.), *New meanings of death*. New York: McGraw-Hill, 1977.

9

Core Dimensions of the Relationship

In discussing the core experience of loss, it is very apparent that the responses of the counselor to the topic of loss can strongly affect the effectiveness of the counseling relationship and the outcome of counseling *per se*. Obviously, loss is not the only topic which has an impact on counselors. What we are suggesting here is that counseling is so much more than a linear relationship in which one person, who is skilled, attempts to help another, who is having difficulty with a problem. This linear view implies a one-way influence model and, as we have seen, this model is simply inadequate for an understanding of the counseling relationship; in reality, the client influences the counselor as much as the counselor influences the client (Danzinger, 1976).

The mutual-influence model of counseling encompasses the concepts of the counselor being influenced by learned manipulations of the client and of the counselor reinforcing the very behaviors in the client which are maladaptive. This model encompasses the effects of the content of the sessions on the counselor *and* the client.

At Level One in the counseling relationship the content of what is expressed can have an impact on the counselor. When it does, we say that the counselor has been "hooked" by content and is reponding to that rather than hearing how the content of the client's life is affecting the client.

At the second level of communication in counseling, the counselor can be "hooked" by the affect which is expressed, primarily in a nonverbal mode and in subtle ways that we have all learned socially. It is when the counselor allows him/herself to be manipulated by these cues that s/he tends to reinforce maladaptive behavior.

At core levels of communication, the counselor is susceptible to influence from many sources. Content which describes core experiences (like loss) can trigger unresolved experiences in the counselor; strong nonverbal cues can cue sympathy, distance or other strong affect in the counselor; and the relationship between counselor and

101

strong affect in the counselor; and the relationship between counselor and client has its strongest mutual influence during core levels
of communication – the I/thou of relationship described by Patterson (1974).

For example, the client may be talking about a sexual problem
with his wife. The topic may generate in the client feelings of uneasiness aroused by the act of talking about sex, feelings of anger at
his wife, feelings of ambivalence about his marital relationship, etc.

The counselor, understanding the content, may feel threatened,
because the problem is similar to one she had with her husband years
ago – or even currently; she may feel irritated, because the client's
reactions to his wife seem childish, and/or she may feel bored, because the sexual problem has been the client's favorite topic for the
last eight sessions.

At another level, the counselor may pick up on the nonverbal
cues which indicate anger, uneasiness or ambivalence, or all three
and, depending on her social experience with those cues, she can be
affected by them.

And, at the core level of communication, how the client and
counselor feel about one another can have an impact. The sexual
topic may arouse sexual feelings toward the counselor in the client
(and what interesting nonverbal cues would be sent at this point
to complicate the issue!) and sexual feelings in the counselor toward
the client . (Yes, counselors send out cues, too!)

CONTENT as a REFLECTION of PROCESS

The last feeling generated is a clear example of the interpersonal
process between client and counselor. It is also a clear example of
metacommunication.

1. *Metacommunication*. This term is used to describe situations where the content of the session reflects a relationship concern between counselor and client. Because we are used to speaking
indirectly about our concerns, we often employ this method of communicating about communication. Danzinger and others maintain
that every statement we make is a *definition*. Whether the statement
concerns the weather or how we feel about each other, it communicates that we feel we are in a relationship where we *can* discuss the
weather or our feelings for one another. In essence, we define our relationships every time we speak.

Danzinger (1976) and Haley (1967) both assert that a frequent
use of communication is to send indirect messages to the listener. Metacommunication responses by the counselor, a form of interpretation, focus specifically on the interaction between counselor and cli-

ent, bringing the discussion to the here-and-now as no other response can. It is difficult and challenging to the counselor, for s/he has to be able to discriminate between client statements which actually do reflect some problem in the counseling relationship and those which represent, at face value, the concerns of the client. There is, of course, a danger in over-interpretation of metacommunication. It is preferable to err on the side of accepting the face value meaning in the client's remarks than to risk diverting the client from his/her train of thought. However, the counselor and client can benefit, on selected occasions, by focusing on their own interaction. And the counselor can benefit from frequently considering the possible validity of his/her client's remarks when applied to the counseling relationship. The counselor can often see and understand the kind of messages that both partners have been sending and how they are received. In some ways, the client may be duplicating his/her views of his/her relationships in the counseling session (Haley, 1967). The counselor needs to be aware of repetitive behaviors or themes which may also be occurring in the client's real world. Metacommunication is a reciprocal communication, meaning that it can be reflective of the counselor-client relationship and of the client's interactive style at the same time.

| Example: | Client: | . . . He makes me so mad . . . |
| | Counselor: | For some time now you've been talking about people who make you angry. It sounds like you're very angry at me. |

Example:	- - - - - - - -	
	Counselor:	While you were talking just now about how helpless you feel with your teachers, it occurred to me how helpless you've been acting in here.
	Purpose:	Relates current interaction between counselor and client to client's style.

2.   *Internal Mirroring.*   Internal mirroring occurs when a relational issue between client and counselor becomes the content of the session and it is reflective of the relational concerns the client has in the "real world;" that is, in the client's life outside the counseling session.   Occasionally clients cannot or will not talk about the problems in their lives (This seems to be particularly true of compulsory clients.) and continue to insist that they have nothing of concern to talk about.   The counselor continues to listen to whatever content is presented and "out of a clear blue sky" the counselor is suddenly engaged in a struggle to gain the client's trust, or s/he is the recipient of

apparently unprovoked hostility or dependency. At least a portion of this development is a reflection of something which is going on elsewhere. It is the sensitive counselor who can plug in the bits and pieces of the scanty content s/he has listened to and relate it to what is going on in the immediate moment between counselor and client.

> Example: Client: No matter what I ask you or how I phrase the question, you won't give me any answers. I'm sick and tired of your wishy-washy responses!
>
> Counselor: I think you're sick and tired of no one giving you any answers and having to find your own solutions to everything.
>
> *Purpose:*   Relates current interaction between client and counselor and client's unexpressed concerns.

3.   *Interpretation.*   Both of these responses clearly call for a kind of interpretation on the part of the counselor. Interpretive responses made by the counselor require an ability to think creatively. Levy (1963) said that interpretation is simply putting content together to form a new picture. It is always better, of course, for the client to develop his/her own new pictures, but there are times when the counselor can be helpful in moving past repetitive thinking and patterns suggesting another way of looking at the data. There are two key *guidelines* about interpretation. One is that it should be given with a light touch. Interpretation is *not* the stereotyped Freudian-psychoanalytic tradition of pronouncements from a god — i. e., "You are saying you love your wife, but it is obvious your wife represents the security of the mother's womb, which you wish to return to." A lighter touch would suggest (if content and feelings indicated such an interpretation): "Sometimes I feel you are talking more about your mother than your wife." In this example, the counselor is owning the hunch s/he has, leaving the client free to accept or reject the interpretation.

This suggests the second guideline for use of interpretation: An interpretation is only as good as its acceptance. That is, no matter how brilliant the counselor may think his/her new connection may be, if the client does not "buy it," it is not worth the breath to say it, and one should move on quickly to something else — preferably returning to the client's view of his/her world.

Use of interpretations serves two interesting and diametrically opposed relational purposes. When the interpretation is useful to the client and accepted by the client, the relationship tends to become stronger. The reason for this is simple. The client feels good about the knowledge that the counselor truly understands his/her life-space and the counselor is feeling reinforced for the acceptance of the marvelously creative thinking s/he has done.

When the interpretation is off the mark, the distance between counselor and client increases and the relationship weakens. The client feels misunderstood and the counselor often feels: (a) somewhat stupid for missing the data and failing to put it together in a useful manner or (b) that the client is stubborn and resistant.

The RELATIONAL ISSUES

At any given point within the counseling session, a counselor and client experience the *relational issues* (Banaka, 1971) of *inclusion, affection* and *control*. Relational issues are seasoned by the way each member of the relationship feels about him/herself as well as how s/he feels about the other member of the relationship. They are alluded to indirectly at metacommunication levels of communication, yet they are also present even when not indicated at all by direct or indirect expression of content.

1.   *Inclusion.* Inclusion indicates commitment to the working relationship — how "in" or "out" of the relationship each participant feels.   Counseling is a mutual responsibility, and whenever one member assumes total responsibility for the direction of the interview the amount of inclusion and involvement felt by the other member will be reduced. Distancing responses by the counselor may contribute to the client's feeling less involved. Presence in the client of feelings that little or no progress is being made will also lower the client's commitment to the relationship and increase his/her feelings of exclusion.   Counselors are frequently able to infer the client's lowered level of inclusion by missed appointments, lack of progress, lack of new material being introduced, rapid changes of topics and apathetic responses.   All of these behavioral examples can be interpreted from one school of thought, as signs of resistance, yet if we consider the sequence of behaviors between client and counselor which sparked the resistance, we can usually see that resistance occurs when the counselor is either pushing too hard and too fast or, conversely, has completely misread his/her client. Resistance, then, becomes another word for the client's withdrawing from commitment to the counseling relationship. The client no longer wishes inclusion.

At these points, when the process seems to slow down or get "jerky" and uneven, when behaviors suggest "resistance" and/or lack of inclusion, the counselor can check the client's feelings about the progress being made and the level of involvement by open-ended inquiry about the relationship. A straight answer may not occur particularly in those clients who are laboring with learning how to handle direct communication, but this approach frequently is more successful than questions about the missed appointments. Even more importantly, the counselor would be able to recognize his/her

own feelings about the relationship with the client. As the counselor-in-training increases the awareness of her/his own feelings in
general, without focusing too much on "logical" explanations for
feelings or the appropriateness of feelings, s/he will develop the
ability to recognize internal signals and cues, so that s/he will sense
her/his own reactions and responses to the counseling relationship
as they occur.

For example, a counselor has been working with a twenty-
year-old mother of two for several months. The goals of counseling
have been mutually defined; the client wishes to reduce her dependency on her parents and is apparently making good progress. The
counselor likes the client very much; she has an easy sense of humor
and is capable of much insight. Yet the counselor is dreading appointments with the client more and more. Frequently the counselor's
attention wanders during the hour. Now the counselor can examine
the reasons behind this new development. It may be that the client
reminds the counselor of his/her sister and the relationship with that
sister is under some stress. It is this similarity which is being carried
over into the counseling relationship. Or by digging further, the
counselor may find that s/he is really angry at the client for her rapid
progress; a sure sign that she will not be needing him/her much
longer. These pursuits into the *why* of the counselor's feelings may
in fact be profitable in further developing self-understanding and in
improving his/her overall functioning as a counselor. However,
they may not be helpful to this client at all. Or the counselor can
identify the actual feelings that are occurring, which in this case seem
to be dread and inattention, and try to connect those feelings to *what*
is going on in a practical and immediate sense. In this particular case,
the counselor's appointments were scheduled for four o'clock on
Friday afternoons and simple fatigue was the "what" of the interpersonal dynamics.

The difference between what is happening and why someone
feels the way they do is subtle yet crucial for our purposes. We may
not be able to *do* anything about a client's resemblance to a relative,
and recognition of the resemblance rarely changes the emotional
response. Yet if we know a patient's whining — a specific behavioral
or situational act — is followed by feelings of distance in the counselor, we may be able to work with the two responses within the relationship. *Why* the counselor reacts to whining in this manner is
another interesting question and may be due to multiple factors,
very few of which are pertinent to this particular client; yet it may
be relevant for this counselor to know *what* responses the client's
behavior elicits in others when these responses are inhibiting the

development of the relationship. (It also should be noted, for the purposes of this example, that whining usually elicits the "social" response of distancing.)

2. *Affection — Client-Counselor.* Closely related to the feeling of inclusion is the feeling of *affection.* How the client feels about the counselor is always a factor in the relationship which should be kept under consideration — not because the client "should like" or feel positive about the counselor at all times, but because strong attachments to the counselor are often made. The counselor often represents the first real, caring relationship the client has ever had and, because the counselor feels it is nice to be needed and appreciated, s/he unwittingly fosters a dependency in the client which does not encourage growth or termination. The counselor needs to meet many of his/her interpersonal needs *outside* of counseling in order not to fall into the "guru trap." The "guru trap" limits the client's other growth experiences because most of his/her needs are met within the safety of the counseling relationship. If the counselor is continually aware of the client's warm feelings toward him/her and also aware of reasonable expectations of progress, s/he can generally move clients from dependence on the counselor towards interdependence on others. The ethical issues involved in strong personal relationships with clients outside of the counseling setting are centered around the "guru trap." Perhaps here too the question is: Whose needs are being met?

3. *Affection — Counselor-Client.* How the counselor feels about the client is another aspect of the same relational issue. At the end of every counseling session, if not at several points during the session, the counselor can ask him/herself how s/he feels about the client. No counselor can reasonably expect to like *all* clients all of the time, and changes in the positive or negative attraction level occur frequently. The important cues for the counselor are *what* was happening in the interview when the affectional feeling increased or decreased. Did the client reject a particularly brilliant interpretation? Did the client take a piece of advice and profusely praise the counselor for his/her well-timed assistance? Basically, is the client doing what you the counselor, expect and want him/her to do?

DEALING with RELATIONAL ISSUES — Social Response

Banaka (1971) describes some typical ways of dealing with relational issues. As they are emotional reactions, they are not usually clearly included in verbal communications among adults. Children, however, seem to be much more direct in dealing with relational issues. Phrases like, "I don't want to be your friend," and "I like you better than anybody," and "You're always bossing people around," directly express issues of inclusion, affection and control. Adults typically react to relational issues in the following ways:

1.   One or both parties privately discount how they are feeling.

2.   One person perceives a nonverbal reaction in the other, assumes s/he knows enough of how the other person feels, and proceeds without checking out his/her perceptions.

3.   One person is obviously experiencing an inner reaction and the other person avoids it with any of a number of rationalizations.

"It would embarrass him."

"It would make his feelings *worse* or stronger."

"It might hurt him if I give him feedback on how he seems to feel."

"It's up to him to expose a feeling if he has one."

4.   Sensing some tension between them, one person "inadvertently" changes the topic to reduce the tension (Banaka, 1971.)

DEALING with RELATIONAL ISSUES — Asocial Response

None of the typical ways of responding to the sensing of relational issues are available to the counselor in working with clients.

For one thing, to privately discount how one feels during a counseling session is to ignore a large source of data which has been elicited by the client and by the interactions between two people.

The second method of dealing with relational issues, that of assuming one knows enough of how the other person feels, is completely antithetical to the process of counseling — the continual checking and rechecking of perceptions.

The third social method, to avoid the issue in order to "protect" the client, gravely underestimates the ability of the client to learn from more effective ways of communication.

And the fourth social method, that of changing the topic, serves the purpose of reinforcing the belief in the client that feelings are dangerous and should be avoided at all costs.

The asocial repsonse, therefore, brings the relational issue directly into the counseling session. Banaka (1971) believes that "relational issues are resolved by direct confrontation when one or both persons believe tension is high enough to detract from the flow of communication."

Example (1): Client: (Silence)

Counselor: It seems you have become more and
more uncomfortable with me lately.

Purpose: To check out the perceived distancing by
the client.

Example (2): Client: I'm sorry I'm late again. I was on my
way here and I ran into an old friend.

Counselor: I'm wondering how you feel about
our time together.

Purpose: To check out perceived distancing by client.

The activities in this chapter focus on the relational issues of inclusion and affection. Attempt to use the role-playing exercises as
much as possible. Focus on your reactions to the situations and
write down those reactions.

ACTIVITIES

A. *Experiencing Relational Issues*

1. *Experiencing Inclusion.* Reflect on a recent experience in
which you entered a room of strangers. What did you do? How did
you feel? Almost everyone experiences tension or anxiety at the
beginning of the experience. Some convert the tension or anxiety
into assertive behavior; some become quite calm and wait for others
to make approaches and introductions; some become shy and avoid
people by staying on the fringes of the group. The next time you
have the opportunity, join a group of strangers and note how you are
reacting. After a few minutes, find an excuse to leave the room.
Observe the group from outside the room – through a window, if
possible. Note how you feel when outside. Compare your reactions
when outside and inside the group. While in small groups ask the
other members to form a circle. You stand a few feet away. Move
to different vantage points within the room. Move inside the circle.
Where do you feel the most tension? Where are you the most comfortable? Does this suggest anything about your inclusion/exclusion
preferences?

2. *Experiencing Affection – Verbalizing Positive Feelings.* In
groups take turns giving positive feedback to one member about his/
her impact on others. Comments may range from observations of
physical characteristics to ways of behaving to values reflected in
the person's behavior. Keep your comments brief. (One sentence
will provide more impact than several items strung together.) Take
turns being the focus of this exercise until everyone has received

positive messages from everyone else in the group. How comfortable was it? Was it easier to give the feedback or to receive it?

This particular exercise is usually surprising to most of us, as negative feelings of dissatisfaction are more frequently expressed in close relationships than positive feelings of approval. Positive regard is frequently assumed rather than verbalized.

3. *Watch a Stranger.* In a public place where you can watch a stranger for a few minutes, note three things: (1) the stranger's non-verbal behavior, (2) the inferences you make about his/her internal feelings, and (3) your feelings about the role of nonparticipant observer in this situation.

4. *Mirror Images.* Get acquainted with your own facial expressions in a mirror. Try out your happy look, your sad look, your angry look, your confused look, your tired look, etc. What muscle changes can you see in your own face? Repeat the exercise in your group. Ask other members to "guess" what different feelings you are trying to express nonverbally through your facial expressions. Or do the mirror images with one other member and ask for feedback from the group.

B. **Role-playing** *(adapted from Banaka, 1971)*

Good role-playing occurs when you know what you are looking for, and when you, your partner, and the observers are enthused about the practice and relaxed about critiquing each other. Another hint: Keep it brief. Two to four minutes of role-playing is often quite enough. Use of video equipment during this exercise is helpful. Agree on role assignments which are atypical of usual behavior — a usually quiet member plays super-talker, etc. Repeat the following role-play exercises frequently enough to allow two or three counselors to meet the role-played clients. Here are some suggestions which may help you gain the most benefit from the role-playing experience.

(a) Make sure your recording equipment is in working order.
(b) Choose a partner. Discuss how each of you feels about role-playing.
(c) Agree on which criteria you will evaluate at the the end of the role-play. (See specific role-play assignments.)

(d) Act out the role-play. Limit the time to two to four minutes. If possible, have a group member act as timekeeper and stop the role-play after a maximum of four minutes.

(e)   At the end of the role-play, give counselor and client a few minutes to share their reactions to the experience.

(f)   Listen to the playback with the group. What additional perceptions did you gain?

(g)   Discuss overall impressions after two or three members have worked with a specific role-play assignment.

1.   *Role-play: Strong Personal Feelings.* Sometimes the client has very strong personal feelings or opinions about a topic. The counselor tries to give the client enough opportunity to express them. It is a challenge to the counselor to keep his/her own personal feelings or opinions from overt involvement in the interaction. Choose a topic which immediately conjures up a strong reaction in both client and counselor. (Some topics which have worked in the past are abortion, women's lib, school busing and how the client would respond to it as a neighborhood parent, living with someone before marriage, drugs and drinking, homosexuality, etc.)

2.   *Role-Play: Super-talker.* Some people control an interaction by talking too fast and too long on whatever topics appeal to them. This is usually difficult for most clients to role-play. The client should begin with the counselor's first question and give a relevant answer. Before the counselor can respond, the client begins talking on a related topic and keeps going just fast enough and loud enough making it awkward for the counselor to interrupt. The counselor's task is to gain or regain control of the interview and at the same time be aware of how s/he feels about the client during the session.

3.   *Role-play: The Underdog.* Some clients control an interaction by not talking enough. They give brief, seemingly factual, unemotional answers. Nonverbally, they convey either confusion or actual unwillingness to cooperate. Instructions to client: Give only one-to-four word answers. Use "I don't know" if an answer would have to be longer. Try to keep emotionally neutral. Instructions to counselor: Your purpose is to have the client communicate and to maintain the interview for four minutes. Also, focus on your feelings about the client's inclusion in the interview and your feelings of affection for the client.

4.   *Role-play: Sudden Emoter.* Beginning counselors are frequently thrown off-guard when the client spontaneously expresses a strong personal reaction. Instructions to the client: React with a strong expression of either anger or sorrow during the role-play. Instructions to the counselor: Handle the expression of strong emotion as if it were a "real" situation.

5. *Role-play: The Compulsory Client.* Clients who are forced into a counseling situation because of probationary requirements, school discipline problems, etc., react differently than those clients who choose counseling. Client instructions: You are unwilling to be there, uncooperative, and resistant to the counselor. Counselor instructions: Pay particular attention to your feelings toward the client in this situation. Also note if you feel any inner pressure to dominate the client because s/he is a "known" troublemaker and counseling is "for his/her own good."

6. *Role-play: The One-downer.* Clients who express a large amount of positive affection for their counselors can be particularly difficult to work with. Client instructions: In any way you can, indicate your strong admiration for the counselor, and your respect for his/her opinions. Counselor instructions: How does this behavior in the client generate feelings within you of affection and/or distancing responses? Try to place the focus back on the client.

7. *Role-play: The Hostile Client.* The hostile client frequently resembles the compulsory client, but some clients who are not forced into counseling can also be hostile. Client instructions: Express your anger and hostility directly or indirectly (verbally, only). Counselor instructions: Again, pay particular attention to your feelings within the session toward the client and handle the situation as you would with a "real" client.

SUGGESTED ADDITIONAL READINGS

Banaka, Wm. H. *Training in depth interviewing.* New York: Harper and Row, 1971.

Banaka bases his whole approach to counseling on the relational issues of inclusion, affection and control. The examples and activities are fascinating and are well worth reading.

Danzinger, Kurt. *Interpersonal communication.* New York: Pergamon Press, Inc., 1976.

This invaluable text is must reading. Noteworthy for this chapter are Danzinger's Chapter Two and Chapter Six.

Haley, Jay. *Strategies of psychotherapy.* New York: Grune and Stratton, 1967.

Often surprising in his directive approach to therapy, Haley's contributions to the concepts of defining relationship and metacommunication are enormous and should be examined further by the interested reader. He also writes with humor.

Levy, Leon, H. *Psychological interpretation*. New York: Holt, Rinehart and Winston, 1963.

This gem of a book considers interpretation as a pragmatic issue — i. e., if it works, it is helpful and if it does not work, it is irrelevant. Unfortunately, it has not been widely read and there are those who hold too fast to the "validity" of their interpretations.

Patterson, C. H. *Relationship counseling and psychotherapy*. New York: Harper and Row, 1974.

Patterson's approach stems basically from client-centered therapy and makes considerable use of the existing data we have about the importance of selected variables in the relationship.

Strupp, Hans H. The interpersonal relationship as a vehicle for therapeutic learning, in *Journal of Consulting and Clinical Psychology*, 1973, *41*, 13-15.

In this brief "rebuttal"-type article, Strupp focuses on many of the theoretical issues and controversies involved in the relationship concept.

10

Control and Manipulation

In addition to affection and inclusion, the third relational issue is *control*.

The NEED for CONTROL — External

From birth to death our lives seem to be in the controlling hands of others. This seeming control has a realistic origin: Of all the animals in the world, the human has the longest period of childhood, of enforced dependency on others. As infants, we are controlled and directed by our parents. Socialization is simply another word for adults exerting controls on children. Every parent can relate the struggles to "control" the child's hunger so that it will eat three times a day instead of every forty minutes, to "control" the child's sleep patterns so that mom and dad can have a good night's sleep and to "control" the child's bowel movements so that it will relieve itself at appropriate times and places and then diapers can disappear. Often this effort to control the child is exerted under the guise of "teaching the child self-control" but it is control, nonetheless.

Around the age of two, the battle for control becomes more vocal and more direct. The child struggles to exert its control; the parents attempt to maintain theirs. The more violently they struggle, the more each opponent loses. Mom may try asking Junior if he would like to go to bed. Junior practices his power-word "No" and the struggle is on. Most child psychologists, by the way, will recommend not asking the child. The question gives the child an opportunity to flex its "no-muscle" in an arena where the child really cannot win and the only outcome is a stormy battle and a thoroughly miserable end to a probably already difficult day. Instead, they wisely suggest giving the flexing two-year-old the opportunity to use "no" on little things — things that do not allow the child to control the situation, things that give apparent but real control. After all it *is* unrealistic and unfair to expect the child to be in real control of the

situation before the child is mature enough to handle it. The elon-
gated dependency of childhood is necessary. The example of the
two-year-old is particularly pertinent to the lifelong struggle we all
seem to have with the issue of control.

Ideally, the parents give increasing control (and responsibility)
to the child as it matures. Yet at adolescence, control becomes the
battle ground once more — the adolescent demanding (and taking)
more and more control over his/her own affairs, hours, money, appearance, values and goals. The parent makes a last-ditch effort to
exert control over this child once more, sometimes even regressing to
pre-adolescent rules in an attempt to hold on to the fledgling. It is
frequently these very control battles that enable the child to break the
ties which have, up-to-now, kept him/her dependent on the parents.

As adults, we find ourselves very often in the position of the
pacified two-year-old: Our control of our lives and our situations is
more apparent than real. The more complex society becomes, the
less control we have.

The examples are endless. At a basic level, we are frustrated
that weather is outside of our control; at a more complex level, the
very air we breathe is also out of our control: Environmental pollu-
tants increase and no one person seems able to affect a change toward reversing the trend. The need for control of our own lives becomes a battle to control events, things and people. It is no wonder, then, that we struggle so hard to control our children when we
become parents. They have become the only objects anywhere
which seem to respond to our efforts.

UNCONSCIOUS BEHAVIOR

At the same time that we are faced with consciously controlling externals, we find that there are internal behaviors which seem
to need controlling. Whether or not we choose to go with a Freudian
conception of unconscious behavior, there does remain the rather
sticky problem of differentiating between behaviors which are deliberate, under our conscious control, and behaviors which are un-
planned, not understood, and not part of our awareness. Some of
these behaviors are mechanical or habitual, some are impulsive and
leave us with a feeling of bewilderment because we are not quite
sure we know why we behaved as we did or because others seem to
misinterpret our behavior so frequently.

One theory of learned behavior proposes the idea that learned actions are based on neural firings in the brain, and if emotional bases of

learning are intense, the neural firings are short-circuited, not allowing new learnings to take place. If for example, your experience with large, fuzzy dogs has been one of intense fear because during your childhood a dog bit you, then the stimulus "dog" fires the neural pathway "fear," and no new learnings can occur, even if the childhood incident has been forgotten. This theory supports a way of viewing unconscious behavior and also points out the necessity for new learnings to take place, learnings which are perhaps under more conscious control of the learner. For some theorists, no attempt is made to bring the repressed or forgotten memory to awareness, as this is not seen as necessary to new learnings. For others, the focus is on the sequence of learnings which took place and the resulting affect on behavior.

Danzinger (1976), for example, suggests that we have learned at some point that the direct expression of emotion or need is painful and risky and that covert messages are more acceptable. If the original learning has been intense, it may be that the covert messages, utilized to elicit set responses from others, become more important than the original expression of need. The desired result — the elicited behavior from others around us — is more important than what we might have wanted in the first place.

Beier (1966) describes a boy who wanted very much to have his father teach him to ride a bicycle:

> ". . . Though he had asked him many times, his father always seemed to be too busy to teach him. This child had emotionally invested in the thought that if his father were to teach him to ride a bicycle, this desired behavior would prove that his father loved him. Therefore, he insisted that he wanted his *father* to teach him to ride the bicycle, and no one else would serve the purpose. His wish was not fulfilled, and one day the child declared that he no longer wanted to learn to ride the bicycle. He no longer asked his father to help him and he avoided showing any desire to learn the task. Apparently, in terms of our conjectures, he had come to the conclusion that his father did not love him and there was no sense in asking for love."

> "But the observer noted that the boy was now *talking bicycle* all the time, particularly when his father was near, and even placed himself near the bicycles when they were in the yard. The father, who was surprised by the boy's sudden let-up in pressure, actually asked the boy if he still wanted to learn to ride the bicycle. The boy answered, *No.* There was an apparent discordance in the way he declared he did not care for bicycles and the way he acted around them and talked about them. The discordance or ambivalence was the boy's way of finding a compromise between his wish to avoid the unpleasant area (father's rejection) and his

wish, his hope, to still succeed. (Father will love me yet!) His compromise involved subtle ambiguous cues (*talking bicycle* and still being around bicycles) designed to tell his father that he was in fact still interested in learning to ride the bicycle, or, more precisely, in obtaining a show of love. While his verbal declaration that he was no longer interested could be seen as a way to discourage his father from teaching him, it was actually a test, a demand for his father to take the initiative and convince the boy that he should learn to ride the bicycle. The rejected lover always seems to need this extra effort in order to be convinced; ordinary effort is no longer sufficient. This is probably due to the rejected lover's awareness that he is forcing a response; he wants to make doubly sure that the desired response, when it finally comes, comes from the other person's initiative, *from the heart*."

"And yet, while the boy did not take the chance of being recognized for the wish (to be loved by his father), which made him feel vulnerable, he did not let his father know that he was hurting (his *bicycle talk*). He apparently was successful in arousing his father's guilt feelings — after all, he made father come to him. The child's advantage in using covert cues, therefore, is that he can safely communicate his hidden wish and obtain a response (guilt), which indicates at least some concern, rather than indifference. The child successfully constricted the response activities of his father through the emotional climate he created for the purpose of achieving a specific response."

This excerpt from Beier's book is lengthy, yet it clearly points out the chain of interactions which lead to unsatisfying relationships. Consider the chain of events which will occur if the father finally convinces the boy to learn how to ride the bicycle. At that point, the boy has achieved what he has wanted, yet he is left with a feeling of vague dissatisfaction, because in effect he is the one who "pushed" his father into the action. The boy can say, in truthful retrospect, the only reason his father taught him how to ride the bicycle was because he felt guilty. At the same time, the boy can repress from awareness the actions of his own which manipulated the situation to his advantage.

CONTROL as a COUNSELING CONCERN

It can be said, and has been, that many of the goals of counseling are related to taking charge of one's own life, which includes working within the limitations of external controls and includes assuming greater responsibility for (conscious control over) one's behavior. This implies incorporating both the deliberate actions and the hidden agenda, or covert messages, which so frequently color our interactions with others. To a large extent, it also means being able to recognize and "own" our own needs and expectations of others and being able to accept our disappointment (our lack of control) when those needs and expectations are not met.

Part of this overall goal is accomplished by fiat: In the counseling session the counselor gives increasing responsibility for the direction, tone and level of the session to the client. All of the content responses clearly follow the client's direction. By continuing to demonstrate faith in and reinforcing the client's sense of responsibility for his/her decisions, the client comes to believe in his/her own skills. It is a delightful moment in the counseling relationship when the client begins discussing what *s/he* has been doing to change her/his life. (Contrast this with the client who is grateful for all the counselor has done to help her/him.)

RESPONSIBILITY and CONTROL

In order to "give" control in a counseling interview, one must first have it. The counselor must be in the position to give the responsibility. The analogy to our developing adolescent and his parent is appropriate here. If a seventeen-year-old boy walks out of the door and heads for the family automobile and the parent yells after him, "You can use the car!" the parent is making a totally useless statement because the son already has control.

Frequently relationships between counselor and client resemble the adolescent with his parent. Control becomes a covert issue between them, with the client struggling to elicit predictable behaviors from the counselor, behaviors which probably reinforce the very pathology which is the root of the client's dissatisfactions. Again, it must be stressed that the client, like the boy and the bicycle, is probably unaware (at the time) of what s/he wants. The client is simply maintaining previous patterns of interaction. "Hooking" the counselor is another way of saying that the client has control of the counselor. It is crucial for the counselor to not give the socially expected response in order to disengage from the control struggle.

Clients often fear the authority which the counselor represents. For most clients, authority figures – parents, teachers, employers – are the controlling persons who have "prevented" the client from feeling responsible for his/her own life. The counselor implicitly threatens the client: What will s/he want from me? How will I have to change? What will I have to give up in this relationship? The client reacts to his/her fears of the relationship by attempting to control the responses of the counselor: If the counselor is impressed by me s/he will not notice how awful I really am. If the counselor is sympathetic to my plight and the cruelty of those around me, s/he will not expect too much from me. S/he will not ask me to change.

Obviously, this magical thinking of the client can obscure the dynamics of a counseling relationship and render it ineffective. Frequently the magical thinking is not immediately apparent from the client's words.

CLUES to COVERT MESSAGES

Our overt communications are primarily based on a verbal communication mode, which is unfortunate. The overt messages do not often indicate covert control issues. The medium of speech lends itself to a wide variance in interpretation and misinterpretation both by the sender and the receiver. The difficulty in acquiring listening skills lends credence to the difficulty in effective communication. The multitude of meanings which can be attached to words and the complexity multiplied by the act of stringing words together in a sequence, stating these words to another person in a given context with the accompanying nonverbal messages suggest the mammoth size of the problem. The difficulty in understanding another may well be, given all of these factors, too complex to tackle. Fortunately, it is not all that bad. Most of us communicate adequately in daily circumstances; it is only when emotional investments are present, as in a relationship (counseling or otherwise), that messages are confusing. Covert messages are then highly important. Context can often give clues as to the amount of control which is present.

To illustrate this point, consider the impact of "I love you" in the following contexts:

1. Political candidate to the loyal campaign workers who have helped elect him: "I love you."

2. Mother to child upon receiving a gift: "I love you."

3. Client to counselor upon feeling understood: "I love you."

4. Eighteen-year-old boy to seventeen-year-old girl in back seat of automobile: "I love you."

5. Sixth grader passing note to another sixth grader which reads: "I love you."

6. Elderly man to wife on fiftieth wedding anniversary: "I love you."

7. Boy scout leader to twelve-year-old scout while on a hike: "I love you."

8. Woman to woman during a group counseling session: "I love you."

9. Child to pet dog: "I love you."

Are all of these messages the same? Did you immediately assign motives to the speaker upon learning the context? Did the impact of the statement lessen or increase in the various contexts? Can we say that the manifest meaning of the statement, "I love you," can differ from the covert message being sent? Are all of these conscious messages?

The ratio of covert message accompanying the overt message may vary tremendously across contexts. The amount of attempted control — the attempt to elicit a particular response from the listener also varies across context — from minimal, as in example number nine to probably maximum, example number four.

All of us have needs to control our environment, which is extended to include those persons in our environment. It is only when control becomes the central motivation or mode of interaction that ineffective interpersonal relations occur. As Beier (1966) states, "The difference between patient and non-patient does not lie in the fact that one uses covert information to affect others, but in the importance of the need to control others through subtle methods." The straight message becomes too risky; the subtle, covert message becomes the only safe course of action.

At that point, or later, we as counselors frequently see the person in a counseling relationship: While the person is receiving recognition through his/her manipulative responses to his/her environment (i.e., s/he is in fact controlling others through guilt and other covert messages.) the person's basic needs are still not being met. Control, as an issue in the client's life, then may carry over into the counseling session as well.

As an extreme example of this, Haley (1966) discusses a client who fought every session to gain "control" of the interview and of the counselor. The counselor deliberately out-maneuvered the client, thoroughly believing that if s/he, as counselor, became predictable his/her usefulness to the client would end. Eventually, the client "gave up," deciding s/he could not win and winning was no longer important anyway. At that point, Haley states that the client was "healthy." (Do control and winning really mean that much to the healthy personality?) The point to be stressed here is that the counselor was consistent in *not* responding in a predictable fashion.

Dealing with Control Issues in Counseling

A highly useful skill for counselors is recognition of controlling behavior in clients and refusing to get "hooked" by client manipulations. Clients operate frequently without awareness of their manipulative style because they have learned that this style of operating at least meets *some* of their needs. Consider the following exchanges:

Examples	*Overt Message*	*Possible Covert Message*
Client:	I was so depressed after our last session, I seriously considered committing suicide.	You are to blame for me nearly ending my own life. You should feel badly.
Counselor:	Was it anything I said which might have made you feel that way?	Counselor "hooks" into blame message.
Client:	You aren't listening to me. I keep trying to get through to you but you're just like everyone else.	It's your fault.
Counselor:	I'm trying to listen. You're just not making much sense.	Counselor "hooks" into blame message and retaliates, blaming the client in return.
Client:	That's it. What do you think I should do?	I am so helpless that you can solve my problems for me.
Counselor:	First, you need to straighten out your relationship with your wife. Then I think you need to clear up your tax problem.	Counselor "hooks" into one-up position, begins dispensing advice.
Client:	I don't know anything about you. Why should I tell you everything about me?	It's difficult for me to talk about me.
Counselor:	What would you like to know?	Counselor decides to take client "off the hook" by offering to talk about him/herself.
Client:	I've seen six counselors so far and no one has been able to help me.	I'm more difficult than you can imagine. You're not strong enough, etc.
Counselor:	All I can do is try.	Counselor is "hooked" by probable difficulty level; gives a weak response.

A good cue to client manipulative behavior lies in the reactions within the counselor. If the counselor feels defensive, attacked, authoritative, confused, very sympathetic, etc., and is *unclear why*, s/he may well ask him/herself if the interaction between the client and the counselor is based on covert messages and could be characteristic of the client's interactions with others. Again, sensitivity to the counselor's own operating style with clients and atypical reactions to others provide helpful indicators to the counselor. These come with experience and a good sense of self-awareness.

The important idea to consider here is that whenever the counselor reinforces ineffective styles of behavior in the client the counselor is: (1) making the client *less* able to change that behavior, (2) adding counselor weight (which is considerable) as a reinforcer to the incorrect learned response, (3) increasing the client's feelings of dissatisfaction and unhappiness and (4) slowing down the therapeutic process. Control errors are probably the most frequently made in counseling, yet they are also, like any other errors, relatively easy to correct and adjust for in later sessions. Recognition is the first step.

It is important to note here that recognition may be hampered by the counselor's own problems with control. Controlling others as a style of interaction is not limited to those who seek professional help. Not only is control an issue in clients, it is an equally crucial issue in counselors. Counseling styles which assume what is best for clients, styles which allow the client little freedom to explore his/her area of concern or to grow without the continual benevolent intervention of the counselor are styles which are characteristic of counselors with high needs for control. Counselors may also need to believe that the client and the counseling session are predictable and therefore easily understood, particularly at early points in the counselor's career. A fairly common example of this is the counselor who plans beforehand what will be discussed in the counseling session. Operating from a "one-up" or authoritative position is typical of counselors who have not yet worked out their own control problems. This will seriously hamper their ability to recognize control problems in others.

We began this chapter with a slight dip into unconscious motivation. We wish to stress that again here with the following statement: A client's reality is the only reality a counselor has to work with. If a client has behaviors which are manipulative, it is very likely that the client is no longer aware of what s/he is doing or why s/he is doing it. The original learning involving the high risk of overt messages and the resulting "necessary" covert messages may be long forgotten. The counselor may choose to work to bring those to awareness or not, but s/he need not reinforce them as significant others perhaps have reinforced them. We are not trying to suggest that you become a "doubting Thomas;" just that you become aware of your behavior in the counseling interview and its inhibiting effects on client growth. Suggested readings in this chapter's bibliography may also help clarify the concepts of control and manipulation by covert cues and messages.

ACTIVITIES

1.   The Rubber Band Exercise (Banaka, 1971): Stand face-to-face with a partner; raise both hands so that your left palm mirrors his/her right palm and your right palm mirrors his/her left palm. Fingers are extended, but relaxed. Your hands are about two or three inches from his/hers. Do not touch hands during the exercise. Now say to your partner: Pretend there are rubber bands around each pair of hands — your right and my left, and your left and my right. We can move our hands in any way we wish, remembering that we are to pretend that there are rubber bands around each pair. Do not talk for the next three minutes. After three minutes, stop the exercise (by mutual agreement or have someone time you). Discuss with your partner your reactions to each other's movements. Some questions to pose are: Who led? How did s/he lead? How fast did s/he lead? How high, how low, how broad were his/her movements? Did the leadership change? How did it change? How did you react to being the follower? How did you follow? What did you watch while you were following? (For example, did you focus on your partner's eyes, using peripheral vision, or did you look directly at your partner's hands?)

2.   Observe two people talking intensely about any topic. See if you can focus on both manifest content and covert cues in the conversation. (Persuasive messages are often covert.) How do the people seem to be feeling? Is there a difference between the verbal content and the nonverbal cues?

3.   Write responses to the following counselor statements. Discuss these responses in your groups and examine them for control issues. Listen to what the client is saying overtly and possibly covertly and attempt to make the *asocial* response.

(a) Client: You don't seem to be able to help me either. You're just like the other counselor I had.

(b) Client: My parents are opposed to this marriage. How do I convince them that Eleanor is the girl for me?

(c) Client: I've decided to drop out of school before graduation.

(d) Client: (shouting) Everything you've been telling me is just nonsense! No one cares a thing about me. Not even you. You just sit there because you're paid to.

(e) Client: I don't think I'll be coming here anymore. We don't seem to be getting anywhere.

(f) Client: What do you want to talk about today?

* * * * *

SUGGESTED ADDITIONAL READINGS

Banaka, Wm. H. *Training in depth interviewing.* New York: Harper and Row, 1971.

This book expands many of the concepts introduced in this chapter. As well as introducing relational issues, Banaka also presents methods of analyzing the manifest content and the process of the interview.

Beier, Ernst. *The silent language of psychotherapy.* Chicago: Aldine Publishing Co., 1966.

The social reinforcing power of a counseling relationship is fully explored here. Beier is basic to understanding the dynamics of the relationship.

Danzinger, Kurt. *Interpersonal communication.* New York: Pergamon Press, 1976.

The issues of control and manipulation are clarified by Danzinger's approach to communication. The dynamics of interpersonal relationship are well-presented in this book.

Haley, Jay. *Strategies of psychotherapy.* New York: Grune and Stratton, 1967.

Haley deals specifically with the control issue as a pathological style of interaction. At the same time, the interested reader is cautioned that issues of control color all interactions, not just pathological ones.

Lefcourt, Herbert M. *Locus of control.* New York: John Wiley and Sons, 1976.

The concept of locus of control is one of the "hotter" issues in psychology today, with considerable research into its ramifications emerging in every professional journal. This book brings a tremendous portion of that research into one source. The chapters which are particularly helpful in understanding its relevance to counseling are one thru four and seven thru nine.

Watzlawick, Paul; Weakland, John and Fisch, Dick. *Change.* New York: W. W. Norton and Co., 1974.

While the focus of this book is on communication patterns and how to change them when they become indications of pathology, there is a considerable amount of allusion to the control and manipulation dynamic.

Watzlawick, Paul; Beavin, Janet H. and Jackson, Don. *Pragmatics of human communication.* New York: W. W. Norton and Co., 1967.

The work of these authors stems directly from the work of Bateson, and as such, deals very specifically with manipulation as a form of control. See chapters two, three and six.

11

Leverage Responses

The DYNAMICS of LEVERAGE RESPONSES

At the very onset of any counseling relationship, the counselor's basic objectives are to be an attentive, active listener and to communicate the act of listening to the client. The counselor listens to the compressed picture of the client's world and then systematically proceeds to help the client expand that picture. The content is gradually enlarged and explored and the bridge from Level One to Level Two, wherein the underlying feelings are also included in the exchanges between counselor and client, is very smooth. That is, there is no particular signpost for the counselor to make the transition from Level One to Level Two. Some clients may introduce and explore feelings during the very first session; some jump into the realm of feelings within the first few minutes. For many, the very role of counselor gives permission to the client to verbalize aspects of self which are generally socially taboo. No matter what the client's timing is, it is important for the counselor to have an accurate view of that "compressed picture" or s/he cannot communicate accurate understanding and has to rely too much on guesswork.

At Level Three content may well be irrelevant. At core levels of communication the content has been explored, associated feelings have been explored and what we are down to at this point is often not definable in content form. Sometimes it may seem to make no sense at all.

The following exchange occurred during the tenth counseling session. The client is a twenty-four-year-old man who is separated from his wife.

Client: I don't know.

Counselor: (silence)

Client: It seems as if . . . I'm not really sure that that's it.

Counselor: You have an idea but you're not sure you can trust it.

Client: Uh-huh. (nods, starts to cry) I was never sure out loud.

Counselor: Once you said it the doubts were there.

Client: She could hear it, too. She knew. Yeah. Yeah, she could tell. I couldn't express that either, you know.

Counselor: And if you didn't say it . . .

Client: Then I knew it was real. Why does it have to be said out loud? (silence) I like to hear it too. (cries quietly) No one ever told me either.

While this session was going on the counselor had very little idea as to what exactly the client was referring. The intensity of feeling which was occurring made it very apparent to the counselor that it was important to attempt to follow the client's processing and basically, that is what occurred. It was not until a later session that the counselor was able to piece together the meaning that particular session had for the client. He had connected his inability and resistance to tell his wife he loved her with never having been told that he was loved as a child.

There is no intent on my part to assign a mystical, magical quality to these exchanges. Level Three exchanges simply occur at points where the client is (a) actually experiencing some impact within the counseling session, (b) exploring an area with core significance (one which has an impact on many areas of the individual's life), (c) in high cognitive and emotional connection with an experience, (d) finding the missing piece which brings the picture into focus or (e) any combination thereof. Level Three exchanges obviously do not occur in a relationship at every session; nor do they necessarily occur in every counseling relationship. Significant learnings can occur without these types of exchanges. Level Three is frequently reached *between* sessions or even after counseling has terminated. (I suspect this is one of the reasons counseling outcome studies are so difficult to assess.) So the counselor should not attempt to elicit Level Three activity in every client. Level Three should not be made the goal of each or any session. Level Three exchanges *occur* and the types of counselor responses at this stage are slightly more active.

The counselor is not "*doing* something *to* the client to move him/her along" but rather is being responsive at this level to cues from the client that s/he is ready to move. There are two guidelines

as to when or whether Level Three responses should be used at all:
(1) The relationship has developed to a "working" point. (2) Situational events in the client's life (content) have been explored. And
there are two rules of thumb as to their frequency: (1) They should
not be used so rapidly as to "pile up" on the client. (2) They should
be spaced with "breather" periods where the counselor and client
can move to content levels. Therefore, the timing of all these responses is crucial. The client should not feel rushed or pressured in
the interview; counselor responses should not be gauged to the
counselor's convenience but to indications of the client's readiness.
In other words, the client needs to assess the impact of the counselor's words as well as the client's own emotions, and s/he cannot
do that if the leverage responses to his/her own emotions are coming
one on top of the other.

LOGICAL RELATEDNESS

Many of the same dimensions of counseling that are present
in Level One or content responses are also present to a degree in
Level Three, feeling or leverage responses. Logical relatedness is
partially evident; that is, a connection can be made from the client's
statement to the counselor's statements. The flow in the communication occurs between the client's statement and the counselor's
response which directly follows. However, the inverse is not necessarily true: The client is not obviously following the counselor with
any logical relatedness and may even appear to be ignoring the counselor's remarks entirely. The example of the twenty-four-year-old
man at his tenth counseling session indicates this pattern.

As the client nears those aspects of self which are the most
difficult to disclose – core dimensions of personality – logical relatedness in his/her own speech may disappear. It may well be hypothesized that *the closer a client is to affective understanding, the
less formal logic is present in his/her speech.*

Counselor remarks at this stage – even though they are seemingly ignored – are very important. They should attempt to reflect
the essence of what the client is trying to express. Feelings are
named with as much accuracy as the counselor can muster and
paraphrases are frequently used.

"Left-field" responses, or those which do not connect to the
client's previous statement, will clearly indicate how much the client
is, in fact, listening to the counselor. When I have "missed" at these
levels the client will look at me, somewhat puzzled – wondering
what I am doing there – and s/he will frequently become side-
tracked, only to return to his/her concerns with a "louder" message
later on.

"Left-field" responses from the counselor usually arise from a misunderstanding of the content base upon which the previous sessions have been built or from too literal an interpretation of the client's current concerns. I am reminded of the client who went on and on about a window on his/her world and I restated something about his/her bedroom window and received a very strange look.

CHANGES in LEVEL

When the client shifts the level of communication from more peripheral concerns to areas which involve core characteristics of personality, s/he will utilize more feeling words and more personal pronouns. It is imperative that the counselor follow this shift and not stubbornly stay with content at this point. Counselors often rush back to content out of their own insecurities or out of discomfort with the affect being presented. Counselor-generated changes in level are always gradual and usually utilized as "breather" spaces. The analogy to deep-sea diving is apt here: Moving up to content too rapidly can give both participants the bends. The client will feel as if s/he had committed a social faux pas and will hesitate to return to that level of communication a second time.

At the mixed level, Level Two, it is sometimes apparent that the client is ready for further exploration of an area. The leverage responses can be useful to the alert counselor in shifting the level closer to core characteristics, but as a general rule, it is the client's responsiblity to initiate change in level of communication downward and the counselor's responsibility to follow and to provide *gradual* upward shifts when necessary for breathers and at the end of a counseling hour. With the use of leverage responses the counselor becomes a more active participant in the relationship.

DIVISION of RESPONSIBILITY in the RELATIONSHIP

Counselors are active participants throughout the counseling relationship. Despite what may appear to be a passive stance, during the early stages the counselor is an active listener, a non-too-simple task which requires considerable expenditures of energy. The primary task during Level Two, the mixed level, the "working level" of the counseling relationship, is to determine the social reinforcements operating to maintain the client's discomfort and to provide the asocial response which promotes positive movement. At Level Three, dealing with central issues in the client's experience, the counselor is verbally more active and often the responsibility for the direction and movement within the session is shared mutually by both participants. Varying the amount and type of lead is the most common method of assuring division of responsibility so that the counselor is not assuming too much control over the direction the hour takes. The amount of lead, the type of leverage response utilized can be compared to a ladder: The counselor's remarks should aim to move the client to the next rung. The leverage response should be close enough so that it does not arouse unhealthy defensiveness in the client and so that it is understood and accepted by the client. "In determining the amount of lead one must guess at how much the client is willing to admit to himself — most clients, in their own ways will tell the counselor if he is going too slowly or too rapidly" (Robinson, 1965). As the counselor uses leverage responses and moves closer to core aspects of personality, s/he assumes greater responsibility for the session, probably risks interference with client movement and growth — both positively and negatively — and changes the nature of the counseling relationship. Sometimes this can be advantageous, sometimes not. Accordingly, the techniques described in this chapter should be used with discretion and sensitivity.

Leverage Responses

1.   *Reflection of Feeling.* This is a continuing response, inviting further exploration on the part of the client. This technique helps to bring problems and their associated feelings into focus without the client feeling pushed or probed. Inaccurate reflections of feeling serve to distance the counseling relationship because the client feels less understood; s/he feels that the counselor has "missed" the essence of the client's communication. Inaccurate reflections are usually caused by a too-previous leap into the realm of feelings without adequate "building" on content understanding. Accurate reflections occur when the counselor in fact has an adequate picture of the client's inner world.

Example:

Client: I wish I could ask him about my grade in the course, but he seems so busy.

Counselor: It sounds like you feel he has no time for you.

Comment: This response approaches the client's feelings of insignificance.

It can also be pointed out that reflections of feeling can be directed at moving the client down (closer to core characteristics) or up (to content) or maintaining the same exact level of the client's statements. Contrast the following counselor responses:

Example:

>Client: After he left, I felt so lonely.
>
>Counselor: (same level):   You felt so alone.
>   (raising):   You felt by yourself.
>   (lowering):   You felt deserted.
>   (content response): After he left . . . . .

2.   *Reflection of Feeling — Externalized.* Occasionally the situation occurs where a very content-oriented person experiences difficulty in expressing his/her own feeling directly.   As a preliminary to moving into the realm of feelings (which may appear threatening to the client), an indirect approach sometimes proves very profitable, much on the order of a desensitization plan. Particularly if we recall that indirect expressions of feeling are *socially* more acceptable than direct ones, we can see the value of using this approach as an introduction.   This class of responses externalizes feelings in such a way as to allow the client the freedom to explore and focus on his/her own internal responses in a very non-threatening way.   The reflection is stated in general terms or focused away from the client as in the following examples.

Example:

>Client: I haven't heard from my father in two years. My brother lets me know how he is doing.
>
>Counselor: It sounds like your father and your brother are very close.
>
>>*Comment:*   This response allows the client to examine his/her brother's relationship as a prelude to examining his/her own.

Example:

>Client: I really think it's interesting to watch my roommates get so upset about grades.
>
>Counselor: It sounds like grades are important to your roommates.
>
>>*Comment:*   Again, the response of others is examined as a prelude.
>
>Counselor: It sounds like it's hard for you to understand why they would be so emotional.
>
>>*Comment:*   Here the focus is on the client's bewilderment due to emotional expression in others.

3.   *Reflection of Feeling in Depth.* These techniques are limited to advanced stages of the counseling relationship for optimal effectiveness. Simple reflections verbalize or focus on the feeling component of a client's statement. Reflections in depth focus on unexpressed feelings and somehow allude to deeper feelings. They facilitate exploration in depth and at the core aspects of the client, sometimes allowing the client to "mention the unmentionable."

Example:

Client: I've never felt this way about a friend before. She's so easy to talk to, yet I don't understand why I want to avoid her. I feel like I'm actually flirting with her in some way.

Counselor: And your own sexuality with another female frightens you.

4.   *Contrasting.* Frequently two or more messages will come through in a counseling session. Bringing them both to the client's attention is an often-used technique which is intended to push the client toward more accurate self-understanding. Timing, here, is again a significant variable. "Rushing" the client to examine self-contradictions before s/he is indeed ready to do so can result in premature termination, shifting of topics under discussion, long silences, real resentment, and general backing off. Accurate timing can result in a strong movement toward self-understanding and behavior change.

Example:

Client: I'm not interested at all in what she does.

Counselor: That's confusing to me. You say you're not interested and yet you've been following her around in the evenings.

Comment: A fairly straightforward attempt to contrast the conflicting messages given to the counselor.

5.   *Confrontation.* In a similar fashion, yet sometimes occurring with a slight jolt to the client, is the technique of confrontation. The counselor does not oppose the client's opinion with the counselor's own, but confronts the client with the client's own behavior, perceptions and/or facts. Confrontation usually startles the client because of the aggressive component implicit in the statement (Ruesch, 1966). Discrepancies or noticeable omissions usually provide the framework for confrontation. Confronting opportunities may frequently present themselves, but it is the wise counselor who does not overuse this

technique.   Judicious usage will increase the effectiveness of confrontation, and a solid counseling relationship will support the strain which confrontation may cause. A huge quantity of "yes, but . . .s" on the part of the client is an excellent indication that the technique is being overused and the client is not ready to hear.

Example:

Client: If I didn't go over there once a week to the Sunday night family dinners, they'd be at each other's throats.

Counselor: You see yourself as completely responsible for everyone in your family. What a lot of power you have.

Example:

Client: And the boss finally gave me a pat of recognition after all this time. It's as if I am finally getting somewhere.

Counselor: Okay. So isn't it time we quit avoiding the subject of your wife?

6.   *Forcing Insight - I.* The label for this particular technique stems from the work of Snyder (1945) and the research by Frank and Sweetland (1962). These responses are not really forcing, they simply focus on a cause and effect sequence by giving the client either the cause or the effect and asking for the missing element. There is a tendency for these responses to generate verbalized uncertainty, understanding, insight and some assumption of responsibility for problem-solving in the client.

Example:

Client: I just couldn't concentrate that year. I hated being in the classroom and I hated studying by myself. I just couldn't hack it.

Counselor: What do you think was causing this reaction?

or

Counselor: I wonder what was going on with you?

Comment: If the counselor thinks the reasons may be helpful to the client, the first reponse may generate further exploration of those reasons. The second response is less controlling.

7.   *Forcing Insight - II.* Again, the work of Snyder and Frank and Sweetland strongly suggests the usefulness of this group of leverage responses.   Understanding and insight show a sharp increase in the client following this counselor response. "Here, the client is given both elements of a cause-and-effect relationship . . . . . The difference between forcing insight and interpretation is in the motivation of the therapist, viz., that of trying to keep the initiative with the client."

Example:

> Counselor: I wonder if there's any relationship between your headaches and your fear of people.
>
> > *Comment:*   The option is left with the client to figure out if, in fact, there is a relationship.

8.   *Self-disclosure.*   As discussed in previous chapters, the counselor who is visible to his/her clients best exemplifies congruency and genuineness and facilitates further self-disclosure on the part of his/her clients.   Research (Giannandrea and Murphy, 1973; Simonson and Bahr, 1974; Doster and Brooks, 1974) has indicated that self-disclosure is most effective when it is brief, does not detract from the client focus and is not done too frequently.

Example:

> Client: When my mother divorced my father I felt like she had abandoned us kids.
>
> Counselor: I know what you mean. I felt like that when my mother left, too.

Obviously, self-disclosures should not be contrived or stretched to fit the client's situation. Notice the differing focus in the the negative examples of self-disclosure below.

Example:

> Client: When my mother left my father I felt as if she had abandoned us kids.
>
> Counselor: Oh, for sure. My mother didn't even tell us she was going. We were six, nine and eleven years old and one morning we woke up and she was gone. Just like that. We felt awful. I can remember my little sister crying for hours. My poor father tried to fix us breakfast and nobody felt like eating . . . . .

Example:

Client: My father died Tuesday.

Counselor: My father died when I was about your age and I felt awful, too. But I got over it.

ACTIVITIES

1.   Invent two or three statements that clients might say in a counseling relationship and write them down. Pool and distribute these statements to your groups and write leverage responses to each. Share your responses and discuss them as to the type of responses and what might be done in a real situation. When in doubt, role-play the written statements and suggested responses and discuss the effects of each response on the client. Pay particular attention to those responses which seem to stop the flow of communication.

2.   Prepare a message that shows self-contradiction as explained in leverage response, number four, *Contrasting*, and hand the exercise in to the instructor.

3.   Tape an interview with a member of your group. Select a member whom you have had (a) little or limited opportunity to know, (b) some difficulty communicating with in the past few weeks, and/or (c) reason to believe is very different in values and personality from yourself. As counselor, listen to him/her discussing his/her life style of relating to others (peer relationships) and what s/he looks for in friendships. Focus on content (using content responses) until you believe you have an adequate understanding of his/her approach to others. Then use some of the leverage responses to move the discussion to Level Two. If successful, be sure to end the interview with content again. While taping, be aware of your feelings toward the client. What could you do to improve the relationship and communication between you. Also be aware of what your client is saying. Can you understand him/her? Can you see his/her approach to others? How does it differ from yours?

4.   Repeat the exercise, as the client. Explain to your counselor what you look for in selecting friends, what things cause your friendships to grow or not to succeed. After your session: How did you feel about your counselor? Did you feel s/he was trying to understand your way of relating to others? Was there any change in how you felt about him/her as a result of the interview?

5.   Discuss the exercise in your group. What factors did each of you notice that seem common to most members of the group? What made your reaction unique?

SUGGESTED ADDITIONAL READINGS

Doster, Joseph A. and Brooks, Samuel J. Interviewer disclosure modeling, information revealed, and interviewer verbal behavior, in *Journal of Consulting and Clinical Psychology*, 1974, *42*, 420-26.

Results of this research indicate that both positive and negative therapist self-disclosure had positive affects on the amount of client self-exploration.

Giannandrea, Vincenzo and Murphy, Kevin C. Similarity self-disclosure and return for a second interview, in *Journal of Counseling Psychology*, 1973, *20*, 545-548.

This research suggests that the use of a moderate number of interviewer self-disclosures may be an effective means of increasing counselor attractiveness and client approach responses to the counselor.

Frank, George H. and Sweetland, Anders. A study of the process of psychotherapy: The verbal interaction, in *Journal of Consulting Psychology*, 1962, *26*, 135-138.

A well-designed study which attempts to delineate the effects on the client of specific types of counselor statements. Counselor responses were found to have a definite influence on client self-understanding and insight.

Robinson, F. P. *Techniques of leading*. Mimeographed version of lecture given at Ohio State University, 1965.

Ruesch, Jurgen. *Therapeutic communication*. New York: W. W. Norton, 1961.

Still a classic in bridging communications theory with psychotherapeutic approach, this book discusses a wide range of counselor responses in terms of how they advance and extend the counseling relationship and counselor effectiveness

Simonson, Norman R. and Bahr, Susan. Self-disclosure by the professional and paraprofessional therapist, in *Journal of Consulting and Clinical Psychology*, 1974, *42*, 359-363.

This is another source of validation for the concept of limited self-disclosure as an effective technique.

Snyder, Wm. U. An investigation of the nature of nondirective psychotherapy, in *Journal of General Psychology*, 1945, *33*, 193-224.

Although over thirty years old, this article represents one of the first attempts to look at counselor responses from their potential effects and usefulness. It generated considerable follow-up research.

12

Integration of Skills and Levels

UNDERSTANDING SKILLS

A skill approach to learning the "art" of counseling may seem sometimes to be awkward and repetitious; yet, it offers the soundest approach to the beginning counselor. The tools of attending behaviors — restatements, minimal encourages, paraphrases and summaries — are all directed at increasing the counselor's understanding of the client. They communicate attentive and active listening to the client and in so doing foster the development of a working relationship. The effective uses of skills aid the counselor in giving the responsibility for the direction of the interview to the client.

Recognition of Skills

At this point, you, the counselor-in-training, should have a reasonable understanding of the role of skills and techniques in counseling. You should be able to recognize these techniques when you hear them used by others and when you hear yourself using them. They may be much smoother at this point and more reflective of your individual style and personality. (It might be noted, however, that the counselor's personality is secondary here. Hopefully, a climate is created where the client is able to express all aspects of *his/her* personality.) Or they may still seem awkward and repetitious. Additional practice using the skills will assist the beginning counselor in developing the smoothness that makes the skills secondary in the session to listening accurately. The skills and techniques you have learned are only tools which promote accurate listening. Sometimes in the process of consciously learning about those tools they become glaringly important and, like the tennis player whose attention is focused on improving footwork and wrist action, the ball or purpose of the practice may appear to be secondary. There is a corollary: Be able to recognize the skills as they are used. The ability to recognize skills also helps the counselor hear what *not* to do.

Questions put people on the defensive; paraphrases need to be accurate to be effective. Silences can be gloriously reflective moments for both members of the relationship or they can be filled with tension wherein the message communicated to the client is that the counselor does not know what to say next. Using a tape recorder with the client's permission, of course, is an extremely valuable activity for a counselor. The counselor can check his/her accuracy, can quickly discern what is being communicated to the client, and can hear what not to do.

UNDERSTANDING LEVELS

At the same time the counselor-in-training is developing skills from the simple to the complex, s/he is probably also developing awareness of levels — both of communication and of personal experience. In fact, use of the skills sequentially parallels the levels which occur in many counseling relationships. The following table shows the use of skills at the three levels of counseling.

Table 1: Blending Levels and Skills

Level One

Content, peripheral, exploratory stages of the relationship (and of the problem)

Content Skills

I   Attentive listening skills (attending behavior, minimal encourages, restatements, paraphrases, summarizations)

Level Two

Mixed, approaching core levels, the working stage of the relationship, characterized by a balance between expressions of content and affect

Content and Affect Skills

I   Attentive listening skills
II   Reflection of feeling
III Self-disclosure
IV   Occasionally, leverage responses

Level Three

Core levels of personality, characterized by more affect than content, close relationship between counselor and client — high intensity

Affect and Content Skills

I   Reflection of feeling
II   Attentive listening skills
III Leverage responses

The basic skills, which comprise the bulk of the emphasis of this text, are applicable and facilitative at all three levels. Reflection of feeling and self-disclosure become basic to the working part of the relationship at Level Two. And at Level Three the additional skills serve to expand understanding at core levels of experience. Recognition of shifts in levels within the client and within the relationship is unfortunately not clearly delineated. There is a "sense" of movement which appears, in exploratory research by the author, to be recognizable by the counselor and observers when it occurs.

Changes in levels are usually initiated by the client; the counselor follows and attends to the proportional affect components of the message. That is, at Level One the counselor uses attending behaviors to expand and clarify the compressed content of the client's experience. At Level Two, the counselor uses attending behaviors and reflection of feeling to clarify and expand the compressed *content and* the compressed *feelings* behind the content. And at Level Three, the counselor uses his/her total repertoire of skills to stay with the client's expanding *affective experience*. At this level, too, the counselor frequently uses his/her own feelings, his/her own sense of the client's experience to further increase the client's understanding. The skills, *per se*, are rarely used to shift the client from level to level but instead follow the client's lead. The one exception to this general client-based direction of the interview takes place near the end of the "hour" (or time spent together). At that point, the counselor can gradually move the level upward, particularly through summarization of feeling and finally summarization of content, so that the time span does not abruptly end with the client still experiencing strong affect without the unifying effects of cognitive understanding and some communication of affective understanding by the counselor to the client.

To summarize then, movement "downward" across levels is generally initiated by the client and supported and recognized by the counselor; movement "upward" across levels is usually initiated by the client but *can* be initiated by the counselor at appropriate points. Counselor-initiated movement in either direction across levels is always gradual (and sequential – Level One to Level Two, Level Two to Level Three). The "plunge approach" to counseling is apparently ineffective and is frequently strongly resisted by the client; the "zip up" to content by the counselor communicates the message to the client that the counselor is uncomfortable with, or even uninterested in, the client's expression of feeling.

CORRECTING for ERROR

The ability to hear changes in levels and to recognize appropriate *and* inappropriate use of skills aids the counselor in correcting for error. Using audio tapes to review sessions with clients is a practical way to continually upgrade one's skills and improve the quality of one's counseling relationships. Even without audio tapes, the counselor begins to hear errors that are made — the wrong emphasis here, the omission there. Errors are frequent in counseling and it is the wise beginner who learns early to accept his/her own fallibility and mistakes. For one thing, the nature of the communicative process does not lend itself well to perfection. We have examined many factors throughout this book which interfere with affective listening and block understanding. And understanding is not a constant. It varies from sentence to sentence, paragraph to paragraph, idea to idea. Mistakes occur frequently because of lapses in understanding. Mistakes also occur because of fatigue, the counselor's mood, distractions, the weather, and *sometimes* because they are supposed to. There are those rare moments when something which Rogers (1967) might have called "organismic understanding" in each of us reacts spontaneously to the client and we spend the next hour or so wondering why we said what we said. We write it off as a mistake only to find that it is one of the most productive incidents in the relationship. In addition, mistakes can be productive because the client will often expend more energy and become more involved in the counseling relationship, just to "help" the counselor correct the errors, or to react to those errors.

There is one more aspect which must be considered in this business of counselor error. In the quest for skill attainment, the counselor seeks some state of perfection that will provide optimal counseling effectiveness at all times. To recognize near the end of a training program that complete attainment is not only not possible but not necessary or desirable can be very disappointing and frustrating to the counselor with a high sense of responsibility for the quality of client outcome. (e. g., A well-programmed computer might be able to achieve complete skill attainment but has not yet achieved any value as a social reinforcing agent.) The counselor's realization of the potential number of mistakes within a session, not to mention within the course of the counseling relationship, can be mind-boggling and s/he might well throw up his/her hands and ask, "Why bother?" The counselor "bothers" simply because, with training, the percentage of quality responses continues to increase over the percentage of counselor errors. The errors *can* be productive, and the counseling relationship which is built on a majority — even a simple majority — of quality counseling responses is highly resilient.

The resiliency of the counseling relationship is easily overlooked. It is almost as easy to ignore as the resiliency of people. And perhaps the real value of counseling experience lies right here. The more we as counselors see our clients as people and the more we understand the kinds of stresses they have coped with, no matter how ineffective the coping style, the more we can see the resiliency of the human spirit. And that simple recognition can lead to the recognition and appreciation of the resiliency of the counseling relationship, notwithstanding the social attributes the counselor has for the client, the mutual transference problems inherent in the relationship and the stress involved in a relationship which is focused primarily on meeting the basic needs and resolving the problems of only one of its members. The counseling relationship can absorb a great many mistakes.*

The SEQUENCE of an INTERVIEW

Several authors (Okun, 1976) have already carefully delineated the suggested sequences of events for a counseling interview. A simplified view might include the following:

1. *Settling in*. The client arrives and is helped to feel physically comfortable. The counselor composes him/herself in an attending posture. Amenities may be exchanged (content) and the client may ask an open-ended question, "How have things been going?" Or summarize the content of the last session, "Let's see, we left off last time at . . . . ."

2. *Content exploration*. The client describes some events (either internal or external) and the counselor assists the client in expansion and clarification.

3. *Exploration in depth*. Usually particular aspects of the session emerge as being significant or representative of the client's concerns. The counselor may recognize these and "focus in" through reflection of feeling, paraphrasing, etc. These central issues, because they are explored in greater depth, have more associated affect (or at least more expressed) than other aspects of the interview and thus may *appear* to be more centrally related to core aspects of personality.

4. *Termination*. This phase of the interview is frequently determined by external factors (job-defined counseling hours, schedules, etc.) so that it is usually the counselor's responsibility to initiate termination. Some clients respond well to a "warning time" ("We only have a few minutes left. Let me summarize what I've been hearing."), some handle more abrupt endings ("When can we get together

---

* As far as I know, no one has yet investigated the ratio of mistakes to accurate responses which will strain and eventually break the counseling relationship.

again?"), some will tell *you* when they have had enough. The summary method is almost invaluable to the counselor: It allows the counselor to paraphrase content, to summarize expressed and unexpressed feelings, to pinpoint areas which seem unclear and which could be talked about next time. It seems to be the most effective method of bringing the time span to a close and bringing the level of the session "up." There is a "termination phenomenon" which occurs with many clients during the last five minutes. The total hour may have been meaningless and during the last five minutes the "core concern" will "pop out." An example of this is a client who spent fifty-five minutes telling her counselor about a dinner party she gave and dropped just enough tidbits of feeling so that the counselor followed blithely along (or as much as the counselor's meandering attention permitted). Five minutes (*exactly* five in this particular case) before the hour was due to end, the client said she had received a "Dear John" letter from her boyfriend and then she broke into tears. The counselor felt extremely frustrated at this point. There is not much that one can do to be supportive or to assist in clarification and expansion in five minutes. The frustration is alleviated considerably if the counselor considers the dynamics of "termination phenomenon."

(a) The client could be attempting to simply prolong the interview (control issue).

(b) The client could be frightened of the clarification and expansion and could be attempting to control the length of time the counselor has to deal effectively with this concern (control and inclusion issue: the client is maintaining some protective distance here).

Awareness of these possible dynamics often helps in resolving the double-bind the counselor feels with the "termination phenomenon." And five minutes may be longer than it appears at a first panicky glance. The same rules for effective listening apply no matter if the time-span is fifty-five minutes or five minutes.

The SEQUENCE of a COUNSELING RELATIONSHIP

There may be some parallel, if I can be allowed to stretch some points, among the book's sequence, the interview sequence *and* the sequence of a counseling relationship. In all three the level goes from a content basis to affective kinds of learning to some sort of summary cognition process. Specifically, however, the counseling relationship *can* include the following phases, which may overlap and may repeat themselves.

1.   *Gathering Content.*   Initial stages of the relationship generally are utilized to gather (and store) a great deal of information about the client. Content responses are utilized during this phase.

2.   *Understanding the Client.*   Overlapping with gathering content, this phase is characterized not only by the counselor's use of (content) responses which communicate understanding but by significant increments in the quality of the relationship because the client believes s/he is being listened to in a non-judgmental manner and is being understood.

3.   *Exploration of Feeling.*   The feelings associated with the content, when introduced by the client and/or accurately reflected by the counselor, are expanded and clarified during this phase. (Again, the overlap with understanding the client is probably inevitable.) One of the most common errors during this phase is lack of expansion. The counselor often has one "good" feeling, latches on to it, reflects it beautifully and then smugly goes on. As we have seen, there are multiple and sometimes conflicting feelings associated with almost every incident.

4.   *The Working Phase.*   Very similar to exploration in depth during a single interview session, this phase of a relationship, again overlapping, explores particular issues which seem to be representative or significant. Clients, by affective cues and repeated emphasis, will point out these issues, or critical incidents, along the way, and the counselor uses these signposts to assist in the determination of areas to focus on and to explore in depth.

5.   *Core Concerns.*   This phase may be a bridge from the working phase or may be absent altogether. The client almost always makes the connection between an emphasis area that the counselor has focused on and a core concern of the client's. That is, the client — through insight or self-exploration between sessions (one or more) or whatever — will trigger these core concerns and "lead" the counselor through this phase.

6.   *Changing Perceptions.*   Again, the overlap is noticeable here. Often, the major value of counseling is in the client's developing new ways of viewing him/herself, his/her experience and the world. The counselor can reinforce these new perceptions by being especially attuned to their emergence by restating them often.

7.   *Changing Behaviors.*   With changes in perception come changes in behaviors — a difficulty. A difficulty because most external reinforcers of the client do not really support changes. A system fights very hard to maintain itself and changes in one member

of a system tend to disrupt the patterns of the whole. Frequently, the other members of the system may expend energy and actual punitive behaviors on the client — the member who is changing. The counselor's role during this phase is to be supportive. It may be the only support system the client has for awhile, particularly if the client cannot gain acceptance in his/her old system and has to develop new ones. (The example that seems most glaring here is the stress placed on many women whose self-perceptions change and whose partners cannot tolerate the role-change which then occurs.) The overlap during this phase of a relationship is quite circular: The client may return to content, to need for understanding, to core concerns and to further change as external responses to his/her efforts to "shift gears" are resisted and trigger memories of ineffective ways of dealing with significant others.

8. *Resolution of Conflict.* The conflicts that are resolved here, during this phase are an outgrowth of change and the way in which change has disrupted the client's social systems. They may be minimal, as when the clients's significant others accept the change, or maximum, as in situations where the pressure *not* to change is extreme. The client resolves these conflicts in his/her own way; the counselor can be fairly straightforward in his/her clarification of the coping styles s/he sees operating, but the ultimate resolution is the client's own.

9. *Termination.* This is basically the last phase of the counseling relationship and may emerge as a specific topic during earlier phases. It may not emerge at all. That is, many clients simply stop coming. Their way of dealing with the ending of a relationship is not to talk about it, but just to end it. A larger majority of clients, however, will need to talk about their feelings at severing a relationship which is often the most significant in their lives. It is at this point that transference dynamics emerge again: The client will project the credit for his/her success (or failure) on to the counselor and the counselor must reaffirm his/her role as listener and supporter. This phase is difficult for both members of the relationship. For the counselor, who by this time probably has developed a considerable caring for the client, there is a loss — a loss not only of the person but of the intimacy, the gratification of watching someone progress in positive directions. The analogy to a graduation — a transition to adulthood out of a dependency relationship is meaningful here. No one continues to grow into adulthood when kept a child; no one continues to learn about reality if s/he remains in the protective environment of school. Strassberg and his associates (1977) have found that there is a point when enough is

enough. Beyond twenty sessions there is no increment in rate of improvement in clients. The idea of a shorter number of sessions (as opposed to traditional ideas of long-term psychotherapy) is consistent with research and with the theoretical approaches of communications therapists (Haley, 1973). Strassberg's findings would seem to indicate that the counselor should consider introduction of the termination phase when the twenty session limit has been passed and if the client has not apparently considered termination. This phase may of itself stimulate significant learnings.

The ROLE of the COUNSELOR

A. *The Counselor as Listener.* Research (Truax & Carkhuff, 1967) has supported Rogers' original hypothesis (1957) about the counselor attributes which contribute to the client gain in counseling. Rogers stated that these conditions were necessary and sufficient for behavior change to occur. The sufficiency of these conditions alone for successful outcome has been questioned, yet the necessity of facilitative conditions as prerequisites to positive outcome in therapy has been well supported (Rogers & Dymond, 1954; Shlien, Mosak & Dreikurs, 1962; Truax & Carkhuff, 1964). As Carkhuff (1969) has stated, "All effective interpersonal processes share a common core of conditions conducive to facilitative human experience." As proposed by Rogers, examining them more closely may suggest the strong undergirding *listening* provides. Note the relationship between these conditions and phases of the counseling relationship, and levels achieved through affective use of skills.

Rogers posits that for constructive personality change to occur it is necessary that these conditions exist and continue over a period of time:

1. *Two persons are in psychological contact.* Rogers states that this first condition specifies that a relationship exists. Relationships do not develop without communication and, as has been stressed throughout this book, communication does not occur without alternating speaking and listening activities. It would seem that the more effective the communication, the clearer the giving and receiving of messages, the more effective the relationship.

2. *The first, whom we shall term the client, is in a state of incongruence, being vulnerable or anxious.* In order for the counselor to know that this condition exists, s/he has to be able to accurately receive and interpret the messages being sent by the client.

3. *The second person, whom we shall term the therapist is congruent or integrated in the relationship.* This condition pertains

to those messages sent by the therapist within the counseling session perhaps more than to those messages being received. Yet how does the client know that s/he is being heard and attended to if the counselor is not sending a message that the client's message has in fact been received? Thus the interactional effect of listening is exemplified Ivey (1971) points out that the congruence between nonverbal and verbal aspects of listening are specific, measurable behaviors. Gilmore (1973) discusses the necessity for counselor verbal and nonverbal behaviors to communicate the same messages to the client (to communicate congruence and integration of messages).

4. *The therapist experiences unconditional positive regard for the client.* This concept has been "kicked around" in the literature since it was first postulated by Rogers. It translates into a prizing of the client, a caring for the client as a separate individual. Listening, as practiced in close, strong social relationships, communicates a concern for the speaker that may well be the basis for the concept of unconditional positive regard. It certainly would differ from the judgmental listening described by Boy (1974) in an earlier chapter. Consider the feeling that one experiences, almost of exhilaration, upon sensing that one has been truly heard and understood.

5. *The therapist experiences an empathic understanding of the client's internal frame of reference and endeavors to communicate this experience to the client.* Sensitive listening involves more than a mere understanding of the verbal messages sent by the speaker (Boy, 1974). Sensitive listening involves a turning in to the meaning that the described experiences may have for the speaker. Empathy involves correctly connecting the client's emotional meanings to the client's verbal descriptions of experiences (Gendlin, 1974). Understanding is the primary task of the counselor, regardless of his/her theoretical orientation, and a prerequisite to planned behavioral intervention. Neither empathy nor understanding can occur without attentive listening.

6. *The communication to the client of the therapist's empathic understanding and unconditional positive regard is to a minimal degree achieved.* In other words, the client at some level must believe that s/he is being heard. The counselor's task, then, is not only to listen effectively, but to communicate in some way to the client that s/he is listening effectively and without judgment.

Carkhuff and his associates have expanded Rogers's original constructs and conducted voluminous research which supports their usefulness to counselors. In summary, Carkhuff (1966) has found that:

". . . . . clients of counselors who offer high levels of the facilitative conditions of empathy, respect, and concreteness as well as the more action
and action-oriented conditions of genuineness and self-disclosure and confrontation and immediacy improve while those of counselors who offer
low levels of these conditions deteriorate."

B. *The Counselor as a Person.* We have pointed out earlier that
a counselor is more than a bag of tricks, more than a collection of
skills. There are many of us in the profession who are "hooked" by
that premise and believe that we have to be supermen with knowledge and perceptions beyond the scope of the average mere mortal.
With the pressure to be a spectacular resource for our clients we use
gimmicks and theories which promise instantaneous cures. Occasionally, we assume responsibility for our clients' lives and enjoy glorious
moments of testimony and a few quiet disasters.

But counseling is obviously more than a gimmick, it is hard
work. The effort involved in working with a client to clarify communication, to change perceptions, to live with situations which may
not be changeable is often just plain tedious. The rewards are not
as frequent as counselors would prefer. Frequently, clients do not
return to advise the counselor that their lives have improved. Grati-
tude is not the typical outcome of counseling.

Counseling can also generate feelings of hostility in the client,
as the act of helping generates mixed emotions in the person being
helped. If the counselor has the goal of changing the client in some
way, teaching him a better mode of operation, s/he can inadvertently
communicate a superior attitude, a "one-up" position to the client
(Brammer, 1973). After all, if the teacher has all the answers how inadequate the student can feel! The very act of communicating all
one's faults and social errors to another human being can cause resentment within the client. It is as if in some cases, the counselor
has become the depository of all the client's bad qualitites and, for a
period of time at least, the counselor is disliked as much as the flaws
which have been confessed. The counselor whose motives for being a
helping person are not clearly thought out can cause more damage
through mishandling of client resentments and normal attitudes than
no counselor at all.

The goal of all counseling is for the client to help him/herself,
not to be primarily the recipient of a benefactor's aid. The goal is
best achieved by counselors who recognize their own limitations,
their own shortcomings, their own blind spots. In a word, counselors
must be human.

C. *The Counselor as Learner.* Counseling is a challenging field
and if any one theory were totally successful with all types of clients,

that one theory would be advocated by every counseling program in the country. Obviously, there are personal attributes which assist the counselor in his/her effectiveness and a few basic skills which seem to be fundamental across counseling styles and theoretical approaches. But new information is made available constantly; new theories are being tried in research programs and additional counseling techniques and skills are being proposed which are more effective with certain types of clients than those which counselors are using now. A counselor must continually read and expand his/her own knowledge of the field.

Most of the books listed in the bibliography are good sources for the beginning counselor. (And oddly enough, after twelve years in this area I feel like more of a beginner now then when I started.) As well, there are several fine professional journals which help to keep the counselor abreast with his/her profession. (These journals are ones which I have found to be particularly useful: *The Journal of Counseling Psychology*, *The Journal of Consulting and Clinical Psychology* and *The Personnel and Guidance Journal*.)

D. *The Counselor as Researcher*. The idea of research causes most students and professional counselors alike to throw up their hands in despair, particularly if the bugaboo word "statistical" is included in the suggestion. However, there is a very great need for counselors to check their own effectiveness. The progress of their own clients, the usefulness of particular techniques, and research on counseling outcomes are ways to tap this information.

E. *The Counselor as Professional*. All of the counselor roles contribute to the professionalism a counselor maintains. Continually working toward improvement of listening ability, maintaining and upgrading one's skills through appropriate learning activities and utilizing research — both the findings of others and direct research into counseling outcome and process — contribute to the professional stance of a counselor. In addition, we have touched upon the ideas of confidentiality, ethical behavior and competence at several points throughout this book. For further guidelines as to professional and ethical behavior, the Standards for Providers of Psychological Services (APA), the APA Ethical Standards of Psychologists, and the APGA Standards are extremely helpful and represent the concerns and objectives of other professionals in the field. They are reprinted in the Appendix.

Like a full circle, all professionalism and professional issues come back to the person him/herself. The counselor needs more than counseling to fill his/her life.

A counselor may meet many demands, face many challenges, and therefore needs to have places where s/he can have his/her own battery recharged occasionally. A full life with many opportunities for healthy emotional exchanges (both intakes and outlets) seems to be a prerequisite to the drains of counseling. And when a counselor overloads his/her own circuits there needs to be a place where tensions can be worked through. Counselors frequently believe that they have to have their "head together." I suspect it is more likely that they have to realize that all of us have moments when our resistances are down. It is wiser to recognize those times and do something constructive about them. It is no disgrace to seek professional help. After all, is not that what we tell our clients? On the other hand, constant reliance on another counselor to support our own effectiveness is not the best recourse either.

Gaining the confidence one needs to be effective is not easy. In this course we have focused on specific skills and awareness of our own personality characteristics and attributes through a team approach. Though it has been just one step toward the goal of working effectively with others, it has been a giant one. Keep growing.

FINAL ACTIVITIES

1.   Your final paper for the course is a self-evaluation of your progress during this course – how you see yourself in terms of skills, interest in counseling as a career, strengths and weaknesses. This paper should be informal and should include as much of your personal reactions as possible. (For example, in explaining your inability to master a certain response, discuss factors which may have been interfering in your group, in yourself, and elsewhere, including lack of clarity in presentation or lack of understanding of the presented skills.) Consider the setting in which you will be counseling (school, mental health, private practice, etc.) and estimate the skills you have yet to learn. You may wish to include a brief discussion of how you would acquire additional skills in this field.

2.   Final Interview. You will be assigned a client and a counselor for your last interview. The topic, again, is why you wish to be a counselor. Bring the tape of yourself as counselor plus the first tape you made in the course to the appointment set up for you with the instructor. Contrasting the two tapes may be a productive way for you and your instructor to check your progress.

SUGGESTED ADDITIONAL READINGS

Boy, Angelo V. Clients in the school. In Gail F. Farwell (Ed.), *The counselor's handbook*. New York: Intext Educational Publishers, 1974.

Boy fully describes the counselor's role in the school setting. He discusses some of the qualities that a school counselor might particularly need.

Brammer, Lawrence M. *The helping relationship*. Englewood Cliffs: Prentice-Hall, 1974.

This excellent book covers many of the issues about process in counseling as well as provides a good review of skills. The emphasis on "helping" may be somewhat misleading in terms of the counselor's role.

Carkhuff, Robert R. and Berenson, Bernard G. *Beyond counseling and therapy*. New York: Holt, Rinehart and Winston, 1977.

In the second edition, Carkhuff and Berenson include much of the research which supports their notion of the core conditions of therapy. Note the emphasis here, too, on the "helping" aspect of the relationship.

Carkhuff, Robert R. *Helping and human relationships*, vol. I. New York: Holt, Rinehart and Winston, 1969.

This is one of the earliest, clearest expositions of Carkhuff's ideas about the core conditions.

Combs, Arthur W.; Avila, Donald L. and Purhey, William W. *Helping relationships*. Boston: Allyn and Bacon, 1971.

This book takes a humanistic approach to counseling and is well done. The emphasis on the counselor as a person with her own motivations for wishing to be a "helper" is excellent.

Corey, Gerald. *Theory and practice of counseling and psychotherapy*. Monterey: Brooks/Cole Publishing Co., 1977.

Corey introduces the counseling student to several theoretical approaches. Of particular value are the chapters on ethical considerations and the counselor as a person.

Gendlin, Eugene T. et al. Focusing ability in psychotherapy, personality and creativity, in *Research in Psychotherapy*, 1968, *3*, 217-241.

Gendlin's focusing concepts may be quite relevant to our understanding of empathy.

Gilmore, Susan K. *The counselor-in-training*. New York: Appleton-Century-Crofts, 1973.

Gilmore approaches the dimensions of counseling through content, purpose and process. There is a large section on the practicum experience during training.

Ivey, Allen E. *Microcounseling: Innovations in interview training.* Springfield: Charles C. Thomas, 1971.

This text is always a good review of the basic skills and a good sourcebook for research ideas on counselor effectiveness.

Okun, Barbara F. *Effective helping: Interviewing and counseling techniques.* North Scituate, Mass.: Duxbury Press, 1976.

Okun's book, one of the more recent in the field, provides a nice blend of skill-building and theoretical support. She recognizes the role of nonverbal communication in the counseling relationship. This is a very useful book.

Rogers, C. R. The necessary and sufficient conditions of therapeutic personality change, in *Journal of Consulting Psychology,* 1957, *21*, 95-103.

Rogers, C. R. et al. *The therapeutic relationship and its impact: A study of psychotherapy with schizophrenics.* Madison: University of Wisconsin Press, 1967.

Rogers, C. R. *On becoming a person.* Boston: Houghton Mifflin Co., 1961.

These three sources together comprise much of the best of Roger's writings. The emphasis in all three is on the core conditions of a therapeutic relationship and on counselor growth and development.

Rogers, C. R. and Dymond, R. F. *Psychotherapy and personality change.* Chicago: University of Chicago Press, 1954.

This book is a further elaboration of Rogers' client-centered theory including some detailed expositions of applications.

Schlein, J. M.; Mosak, H. H. and Dreikurs, R. Effect of time limits: A comparison of two psychotherapies, in *Journal of Counseling Psychology,* 1962, *9*, 31-34.

Indirectly this article provided nice support for the core conditions as prerequisites to positive outcome in therapy.

Strassberg, Donald S. et al. Successful outcome and number of sessions: When do counselors think enough is enough? in *Journal of Counseling Psychology*, 1977, *24*, 477-480.

The findings of Strassberg and his associates seem to support the contention that there is an optimum number of counseling sessions, beyond which there are few if any gains for the client.

Truax, C. B. and Carkhuff, Robert. For better or for worse: The process of psychotherapeutic change, in *Recent advances in behavioral change.* Montreal: McGill University Press, 1964.

Truax, C. B. and Carkhuff, Robert. *Toward effective counseling and psychotherapy.* Chicago: Aldine Publishing Co., 1967.

These writings are the further elaboration and results of research into core conditions.

Tyler, Leona. *The work of the counselor.* New York: Appleton-Century-Crofts, 1969.

Tyler's book is a classic in the field, providing good, stimulating reading, clarification of many counselor roles and elucidation of most counseling issues. This is must reading.

APPENDIX

American Personnel and Guidance Association

*Ethical Standards**

PREAMBLE

The American Personnel and Guidance Association is an educational, scientific, and professional organization dedicated to service to society. This service is committed to profound faith in the worth, dignity, and great potentiality of the individual human being.

COUNSELING

This section refers to practices involving a counseling relationship with a counselee or client and is not intended to be applicable to practices involving administrative relationships with the persons being helped. A counseling relationship denotes that the person seeking help retain full freedom of choice and decision and that the helping person has no authority or responsibility to approve or disapprove of the choices or decisions of the counselee or client. "Counselee" or "client" is used here to indicate the person (or persons) for whom the member has assumed a professional responsibility. Typically the counselee or client is the individual with whom the member has direct primary contact. However, at times, "client" may include another persons(s) when the other person(s) exercise significant control and direction over the individual being helped in connection with the decisions and plans being considered in counseling.

1. The member's *primary* obligation is to respect the integrity and promote the welfare of the counselee or client with whom he is working.

2. The counseling relationship and information resulting therefrom must be kept confidential consistent with the obligations of the member as a professional person.

3. Records of the counseling relationship including interview notes, test data, correspondence, tape recordings, and other documents are to be considered professional information for use in counseling research, and teaching of counselors but always with full protection of the identity of the client and with precaution so that no harm will come to him.

4. The counselee or client should be informed of the conditions under which he may receive counseling assistance at or before the time he enters the counseling relationship. This is particularly true in the event that there exist conditions of which the counselee or client would not likely be aware.

---

* Reproduced by permission of the American Personnel and Guidance Association from an article on Ethical Standards in *Personnel and Guidance Journal, 40,* © Copyright 1961, pages 206-209.

5.   The member reserves the right to consult with any other professionally competent person about his counselee client. In choosing his professional consultant the member must avoid placing the consultant in a conflict of interest situation, i. e., the consultant must be free of any other obligatory relation to the member's client that would preclude the consultant being a proper party to the member's efforts to help the counselee or client.

6.   The member shall decline to initiate or shall terminate a counseling relationship when he cannot be of professional assistance to the counselee or client either because of lack of competence or personal limitation. In such instances the member shall refer his counselee or client to an appropriate specialist. In the event the counselee or client declines the suggested referral, the member is not obligated to continue the counseling relationship.

7.   When the member learns from counseling relationshps of conditions which are likely to harm others over whom his institution or agency has responsibility, he is expected to report *the condtion* to the appropriate responsible authority, but in such a manner as not to reveal the identity of his counselee or client.

8.   In the event that the counselee or client's condition is such as to require others to assume responsibility for him, or where there is clear and imminent danger to the counselee or client or to others, the member is expected to report this fact to an appropriate responsible authority, and/or take such other emergency measures as the situation demands.

9.   Should the member be engaged in a work setting which calls for any variation from the above statements, the member is obligated to ascertain that such variations are justifiable under the conditions and that such variations are clearly specified and made known to all concerned with such counseling services.

American Psychological Association

Revised Ethical Standards of Psychologists

APA Monitor

March, 1977

PREAMBLE

Psychologists[1] [2] respect the dignity and worth of the individual and honor the preservation and protection of fundamental human rights. They are committed to increasing knowledge of human behavior and of people's understanding of themselves and others and to the utilization of such knowledge for the promotion of human welfare. While pursuing these endeavors, they make every effort to protect the welfare of those who seek their services or of any human being or animal that may be the object of study. They use their skills only for purposes consistent with these values and do not knowingly permit their misuse by others. While demanding for themselves freedom of inquiry and communication, psychologists accept the responsibility this freedom requires: competence, objectivity in the application of skills and concern for the best interests of clients, colleagues, and society in general. In pursuit of these ideals, psychologists subscribe to principles in the following areas: (1) Responsibility, (2) Competence, (3) Moral and Legal Standards, (4) Public Statements, (5) Confidentiality, (6) Welfare of the Consumer, (7) Professional Relationships, (8) Utilization of Assessment Techniques, and (9) Pursuit of Research Activities.

Principle One

RESPONSIBILITY

In their commitment to the understanding of human behavior, psychologists value objectivity and integrity, and in providing services they maintain the highest standards of their profession. They accept responsibility for the consequences of their work and make every effort to insure that their services are used appropriately.

---

1. Approved by the Council of Representatives, January 30, 1977.

2. A student of psychology who assumes the role of a psychologist shall be considered a psychologist for the purpose of this code of ethics.

a.   As scientists, psychologists accept the ultimate responsibility for selecting appropriate areas and methods most relevant to these areas. They plan their research in ways to minimize the possibility that their findings will be misleading. They provide thorough discussion of the limitations of their data and alternative hypotheses, especially where their work touches on social policy or might be construed to the detriment of persons in specific age, sex, ethnic, socioeconomic or other social groups. In publishing reports of their work, they never suppress disconfirming data. Psychologists take credit only for the work they have actually done.

Psychologists clarify in advance will all appropriate persons or agencies the expectations for sharing and utilizing research data. They avoid dual relationships which may limit objectivity, whether political or monetary, so that interference with data, human participants, and milieu is kept to a minimum.

b.   As employees of an institution or agency, psychologists have the responsibility of remaining alert to and attempting to moderate institutional pressures that may distort reports of psychological findings or impede their proper use.

c.   As members of governmental or other organizational bodies, psychologists remain accountable as individuals to the highest standards of their profession.

d.   As teachers, psychologists recognize their primary obligation to help others acquire knowledge and skill. They maintain high standards of scholarship and objectivity by presenting psychological information fully and accurately.

e.   As practitioners, psychologists know that they bear a heavy social responsibility because their recommendations and professional actions may alter lives of others. They are alert to personal, social, organizational, financial, or political situations or pressures that might lead to misuse of their influence.

f.   Psychologists provide adequate and timely evaluations to employees, trainees, students, and others whose work they supervise.

Principle Two

COMPETENCE

The maintenance of high standards of professional competence is a responsibility shared by all psychologists in the interest of the public and the profession as a whole. Psychologists recognize the boundaries of their competence and the limitations of their techniques and only provide services, use techniques, or offer opinions as professional that meet recognized standards. Psychologists maintain knowledge of current scientific and professional information related to the services they render.

a.   Psychologists accurately represent their competence, education, training, and experience. Psychologists claim as evidence of professional qualifications only those degrees obtained from institutions acceptable under the Bylaws and Rules of Council of the American Psychological Association.

b.   As teachers, psychologists perform their duties on the basis of careful preparation so that their instruction is accurate, current and scholarly.

c.   Psychologists recognize the need for continuing education and are open to new procedures and changes in expectations and values over time. They recognize differences among people, such as those that may be associated with age, sex, socioeconomic, and ethnic backgrounds. Where relevant, they obtain training, experience, or counsel to assure competent service or research relating to such persons.

d.   Psychologists with the responsibility for decisions involving individuals or policies based on test results have an understanding of psychological or educational measurement, validation problems and other test research.

e.   Psychologists recognize that their effectiveness depends in part upon their ability to maintain effective interpersonal relations, and that aberrations on their part may interfere with their abilities. They refrain from undertaking any activity in which their personal problems are likely to lead to inadequate professional services or harm to a client; or, if engaged in such activity when they become aware of their personal problems, they seek competent professional assistance to determine whether they should suspend, terminate or limit the scope of their professional and/or scientific activities.

Principle Three

MORAL AND LEGAL STANDARDS

Psychologists' moral, ethical and legal standards of behavior are a personal matter to the same degree as they are for any other citizen, except as these may compromise the fulfillment of their professional responsibilities, or reduce the trust in psychology or psychologists held by the general public. Regarding their own behavior, psychologists should be aware of the prevailing community standards and of the possible impact upon the quality of professional services provided by their conformity to or deviation from these standards. Psychologists are also aware of the possible impact of their public behavior upon the ability of colleagues to perform their professional duties.

a.   Psychologists as teachers are aware of the diverse backgrounds of students and, when dealing with topics that may give offense, treat the material objectively and present it in a manner for which the student is prepared.

b.   As employees, psychologists refuse to participate in practices inconsistent with legal, moral and ethical standards regarding the treatment of employees or of the public. For example, psychologists will not condone practices that are inhumane or that result in illegal or otherwise unjustifiable discrimination on the basis of race, age, sex, religion or national origin in hiring, promotion, or training.

c.   In providing psychological services, psychologists avoid any action that will violate or diminish the legal and civil rights of clients or of others who may be affected by their actions.

As practitioners, psychologists remain abreast of relevant federal, state, local, and agency regulations and Association standards of practice concerning the conduct of their practices. They are concerned with developing such legal and quasi-legal regulations as best serve the public interest and in changing such existing regulations as are not beneficial to the interests of the public and the profession.

d.   As researchers, psychologists remain abreast of relevant federal and state regulations concerning the conduct of research with human participants or animals.

Principle Four

PUBLIC STATEMENTS

Public statements, announcements of services, and promotional activities of psychologists serve the purpose of providing sufficient information to aid the consumer public in making informed judgments and choices. Psychologists represent accurately and objectively their professional qualifications, affiliations, and functions, as well as those of the institutions or organizations with which they or the statements may be associated. In public statements providing psychological information or professional opinions or providing information about the availability of psychological products and services, psychologists take full account of the limits and uncertainties of present psychological knowledge and techniques.

a.   When announcing professional services, psychologists limit the information to: name, highest relevant academic degree conferred, date and type of certification or licensure, diplomate status, address, telephone number, office hours, and a brief listing of the type of psychological services offered. Such statements are descriptive of services provided but not evaluative as to their quality or uniqueness. They do not contain testimonials by quotation or by implication. They do not claim uniqueness of skills or methods unless determined by acceptable and public scientific evidence.

b.   In announcing the availability of psychological services or products, psychologists do not display any affiliations with an organization in a manner that falsely implies the sponsorship or certification of that organization. In particular and for example, psychologists do not offer APA membership or fellowship as evidence of qualification. They do not name their employer or professional associations unless the services are in fact to be provided by or under the responsible, direct supervision and continuing control of such organizations or agencies.

c.   Announcements of "personal growth groups" give a clear statement of purpose and the nature of the experiences to be provided. The education, training and experience of the psychologists are appropriately specified.

d.   Psychologists associated with the development of promotion of psychological devices, books, or other products offered for commercial sale make every effort to insure that announcements and advertisements are presented in a professional, scientifically acceptable, and factually informative manner.

e.   Psychologists do not participate for personal gain in commercial announcements recommending to the general public the purchase or use of any proprietary single-source product or service.

f.   Psychologists who interpret the science of psychology or the services of psychologists to the general public accept the obligation to present the material fairly and accurately, avoiding misrepresentation through sensationalism, exaggeration or superficiality. Psychologists are guided by the primary obligation to aid the public in forming their own informed judgments, opinions and choices.

g.   As teachers, psychologists insure that statements in catalogs and course outlines are accurate and sufficient, particularly in terms of subject matter to be covered, bases for evaluating progress, and nature of course experiences. Announcements or brochures describing workshops, seminars, or other educational programs accurately represent intended audience and eligibility requirements, educational objectives, and nature of the material to be covered, as well as the education, training and experience of the psychologists presenting the programs, and any fees involved. Public announcements soliciting subjects for research, and in which clinical services or other professional services are offered as an inducement, make clear the nature of the services as well as the costs and other obligations to be accepted by the human participants of the research.

h.   Psychologists accept the obligation to correct others who may represent the psychologist's professional qualifications or associations with products or services in a manner incompatible with these guidelines.

i.   Psychological services for the purpose of diagnosis, treatment or personal advice are provided only in the context of a professional relationship, and are not given by means of public lectures or demonstrations, newspaper or magazine articles, radio or television programs, mail, or similar media.

Principle Five

CONFIDENTIALITY

Safeguarding information about an individual that has been obtained by the psychologist in the course of his teaching, practice, or investigation is a primary obligation of the psychologist. Such information is not communicated to others unless certain important conditions are not met.

a.   Information received in confidence is revealed only after most careful deliberation and when there is clear and imminent danger to an individual or to society, and then only to appropriate professional workers or public authorities.

b.   Information obtained in clinical or consulting relationships, or evaluative data concerning children, students, employees, and others are discussed only for professional purposes and only with persons clearly concerned with the case. Written and oral reports should present only data germane to the purposes of the evaluation and every effort should be made to avoid undue invasion of privacy.

c.   Clinical and other materials are used in classroom teaching and writing only when the identity of the persons involved is adequately disguised.

d.   The confidentiality of professional communications about individuals is maintained. Only when the originator and other persons involved give their express permission is a confidential professional communication shown to the individual concerned. The psychologist is responsible for informing the client of the limits of the confidentiality.

e.   Only after explicit permission has been granted is the identity of research subjects published. When data have been published without permission for identification, the psychologist assumes responsibility for adequately disguising their sources.

f.   The psychologist makes provisions for the maintenance of confidentiality in the prevention and ultimate disposition of confidential records.

Principle Six

WELFARE OF THE CONSUMER

Psychologists respect the integrity and protect the welfare of the people and groups with whom they work. When there is a conflict of interest between the client and the psychologist's employing institution, psychologists clarify the nature and direction of their loyalties and responsibilities and keep all parties informed of their commitments. Psychologists fully inform consumers as to the purpose and nature of an evaluative, treatment, educational or training procedure, and they freely acknowledge that clients, students, or participants in research have freedom of choice with regard to participation.

a.   Psychologists are continually cognizant of their own needs and of their inherently powerful position vis a vis clients, in order to avoid exploiting their trust and dependency. Psychologists make every effort to avoid dual relationships with clients and/or relationships which might impair their professional judgment or increase the risk of client exploitation. Examples of dual relationships include treating employees, supervisers, close friends or relatives. Sexual intimacies with clients are unethical.

b.   Where demands of an organization on psychologists go beyond reasonable conditions of employment, psychologists recognize possible conflict of interest that may arise. When such conflicts occur, psychologists clarify the nature of the conflict and inform all parties of the nature and direction of the loyalties and responsibilities involved.

c.   When acting as a supervisior, trainer, researcher, or employer, psychologists accord informed choice, confidentiality, due process, and protection from physical and mental harm to their subordinates in such relationships.

d.   Financial arrangements in professional practice are in accord with professional standards that safeguard the best interests of the client and that are clearly understood by the client in advance of billing. Psychologists are responsible for assisting clients in finding needed services in those instances where payment of the usual fee would be a hardship. No commission, rebate, or other form of remuneration may be given or received for referral of clients for professional services, whether by an individual or by agency. Psychologists willingly contribute a portion of their services to work for which they receive little or no financial return.

e.   The psychologist attempts to terminate a clinical or consulting relationship when it is reasonably clear that the consumer is not benefiting from it. Psychologists who find that their services are being used by employers in a way that is not beneficial to the participants or to employees who may be affected, or to significant others, have the responsibility to make their observations known to the responsible persons and to propose modification or termination of the engagement.

Principle Seven

PROFESSIONAL RELATIONSHIPS

Psychologists act with due regard for the needs, special competencies and obligations of their colleagues in psychology and other professions. Psychologists respect the perogatives and obligations of the institutions or organizations with which they are associated.

a.   Psychologists understand the areas of competence of related professions, and make full use of all the professional, technical, and administrative resources that best serve the interests of consumers. The absence of formal relationships with other professional workers does not relieve psychologists from the responsibility of securing for their clients the best possible professional service nor does it relieve them from the exercise of foresight, diligence, and tact in obtaining the complementary or alternative assistance needed by clients.

b.   Psychologists know and take into account the traditions and practices of other professional groups with which they work and cooperate fully with members of such groups. If a consumer is receiving services from another professional, psychologists do not offer their services directly to the consumer without first informing the professional person already involved so that the risk of confusion and conflict for the consumer can be avoided.

c.   Psychologists who employ or supervise other professionals or professionals in training accept the obligation to facilitate their further professional development by providing suitable working conditions, consultation, and experience opportunities.

d.   As employees of organizations providing psychological services, or as independent psychologists serving clients in an organizational context, psychologists seek to support the integrity, reputation and proprietary rights of the host organization. When it is judged necessary in a client's interest to question the organization's programs or policies, psychologists attempt to effect change by constructive action within the organization before disclosing confidential information acquired in their professional roles.

   e.   In the pursuit of research, psychologists give sponsoring agencies, host institutions, and publication channels the same respect and opportunity for giving informed consent that they accord to individual research participants. They are aware of their obligation to future research workers and insure that host institutions are given adequate information about the research and proper acknowledgement of their contributions.

   f.   Publication credit is assigned to all those who have contributed to a publication in proportion to their contribution. Major contributions of a professional character made by several persons to a common project are recognized by joint authorship, with the experimenter or author who made the principal contribution identified and listed first. Minor contributions of a professional character, extensive clerical or similar nonprofessional assistance, and other minor contributions are acknowledged in footnotes or in an introductory statement. Acknowledgement through specific citations is made for unpublished as well as published material that has directly influenced the research or writing. A psychologist who compiles and edits material of others for publication publishes the material in the name of the originating group, if any, and with his/her own name appearing as chairperson or editor. All contributors are to be acknowledged and named.

   g.   When a psychologist violates ethical standards, psychologists who know first-hand of such activities should, if possible, attempt to rectify the situation. Failing an informal solution, psychologists bring such unethical activities to the attention of the appropriate local, state, and/or national committee on professional ethics, standards, and practices.

   h.   Members of the Association cooperate with duly constituted committees of the Association, in particular and for example, the Committee on Scientific and Professional Ethics and Conduct, and the Committee on Professional Standards Review, by responding to inquiries promptly and completely. Members taking longer than thirty days to respond to such inquiries shall have the burden of demonstrating that they acted with "reasonable promptness." Members also have a similar responsibility to respond with reasonable promptness to inquiries from duly constituted state associations ethics committees and professional standards review committees.

Principle Eight

UTILIZATION OF ASSESSMENT TECHNIQUES

   In the development, publication, and utilization of psychological assessment techniques, psychologists observe relevant APA standards. Persons examined have the right to know the results, the interpretations made, and, where appropriate, the original data on which final judgments were based. Test users avoid imparting unnecessary information which would compromise test security, but they provide requested information that explains the basis for decisions that may adversely affect that person or that person's dependents.

a.   The client has the right to have and the psychologist has the responsibility to provide explanations of the nature and the purposes of the test and the test results in language that the client can understand, unless, as in some employment or school settings, there is an explicit exception to this right agreed upon in advance. When the explanations are to be provided by others, the psychologist establishes procedures for providing adequate explanations.

b.   When a test is published or otherwise made available for operational use, it is accompanied by a manual (or other published or readily available information) that fully describes the development of the test, the rationale, and evidence of validity and reliability. The test manual explicitly states the purposes and applications for which the test is recommended and identifies special qualifications required to administer the test and to interpret it properly. Test manuals provide complete information regarding the characteristics of the normative population.

c.   In reporting test results, psychologists indicate any reservations regarding validity or reliability resulting from testing circumstances or inappropriateness of the test norms for the person tested. Psychologists strive to insure that the test results and their interpretations are not misused by others.

d.   Psychologists accept responsibility for removing from clients' files test score information that has become obsolete, lest such information be misused or misconstrued to the disadvantage of the person tested.

e.   Psychologists offering test scoring and interpretation services are able to demonstrate that the validity of the programs and procedures used in arriving at interpretations are based on appropriate evidence. The public offering of an automated test interpretation service is considered as a professional-to-professional consultation. The psychologist makes every effort to avoid misuse of test reports.

Principle Nine

RESEARCH ACTIVITIES

The decision to undertake research should rest upon a considered judgment by the individual psychologist about how best to contribute to psychological science and to human welfare. Psychologists carry out their investigations with respect for the people who participate and with concern for their dignity and welfare.

a.   In planning a study the investigator has the responsibility to make a careful evaluation of its ethical acceptability, taking into account the following additional principles for research with human beings. To the extent that this appraisal, weighing scientific and human values, suggests a compromise of any principle, the investigator incurs an increasingly serious obligation to seek ethical advice and to observe stringent safeguards to protect the rights of the human research participants.

b.   Responsibility for the establishment and maintenance of acceptable ethical practice in research always remains with the individual investigator.

The investigator is also responsible for the ethical treatment of research participants by collaborators, assistants, students, and employees, all of whom, however, incur parallel obligations.

c.   Ethical practice requires the investigator to inform the participant of all features of the research that might reasonably be expected to influence willingness to participate, and to explain all other aspects of the research about which the participant inquires. Failure to make full disclosure imposes additional force to the investigator's abiding responsibility to protect the welfare and dignity of the research participant.

d.   Openness and honesty are essential characteristics of the relationship between investigator and research participant. When the methodological requirements of a study necessitate concealment or deception, the investigator is required to insure as soon as possible the participant's understanding of the reasons for this action and of a sufficient justification for the procedures employed.

e.   Ethical practice requires the investigator to respect the individual's freedom to decline to participate in or withdraw from research. The obligation to protect this freedom requires special vigilance when the investigator is in a position of power over the participant, as, for example, when the participant is a student, client, employee, or otherwise is in a dual relationship with the investigator.

f.   Ethically acceptable research begins with the establishment of a clear and fair agreement between the investigator and the research participant that clarifies the responsibilities of each. The investigator has the obligation to honor all promises and commitments included in that agreement.

g.   The ethical investigator protects participants from physical and mental discomfort, harm, and danger. If a risk of such consequences exists, the investigator is required to inform the participant of the fact, secure consent before proceeding, and take all possible measures to minimize distress. A research procedure must not be used if it is likely to cause serious or lasting harm to a participant.

h.   After the data are collected, the investigator provides the participant with information about the nature of the study to remove any misconceptions that may have arisen. Where scientific or human values justify delaying or withholding information, the investigator acquires a special responsibility to assure that there are no damaging consequences for the participant.

i.   When research procedures may result in undesirable consequences for the individual participant, the investigator has the responsibility to detect and remove or correct these consequences, including, where relevant, long-term after effects.

j.   Information obtained about the individual research particpants during the course of an investigation is confidential unless otherwise agreed in advance. When the possibility exists that others may obtain access to such information, this possibility, together with the plans for protecting confidentiality, is explained to the participants as part of the procedure for obtaining informed consent.

k. A psychologist using animals in research adheres to the provisions of the Rules Regarding Animals, drawn up by the Committee on Precautions and Standards in Animal Experimentation and adopted by the American Psychological Association.

l. Investigations of human participants using drugs should be conducted only in such settings as clinics, hospitals, or research facilities maintaining appropriate safeguards for the participants.

* * * * * *

REFERENCES

Psychologists are responsible for knowing about and acting in accord with the standards and positions of the APA, as represented in such official documents as the following:

American Association of University Professors statement on Principles on academic freedom and tenure. *Policy documents and report*, 1977, 1-4.

American Psychological Association. *Guidelines for psychologists for the use of drugs in research*. Washington, D. C.: Author, 1971.

American Psychological Association. Guidelines for conditions of employment of psychologists, in *American Psychologist*, 1972, 27, 331-334.

American Psychological Association. Guidelines for psychologists conducting growth groups, in *American Psychologist*, 1973, 28, 933.

American Psychological Association. *Ethical principles in the conduct of research with human participants*. Washington, D. C.: Author, 1973.

American Psychological Association. *Standards for educational and psychological tests*. Washington, D. C.: Author, 1974.

American Psychological Association. *Standards for providers of psychological services*. Washington, D. C.: Author, 1977.

Committee on Scientific and Professional Ethics and Conduct. Guideline for telephone directory listings, in *American Psychologist*, 1969, 24, 70-71.

American Psychological Association. *Principles for the care and use of animals*. Washington, D. C.: Author, 1971.

INDEX

Index

Key to notations in the Index:

An asterisk (*) following a page number indicates that the word is defined on that page;
page numbers in *italics* refer to references within the bibliographies accompanying each
chapter; an "ff" following a page number indicates that the subject is continued in the
following pages.